U0502200

每天读一点英文

Everyday English Snack

那些年，那些诗

Those days, those poems

章华◎编译

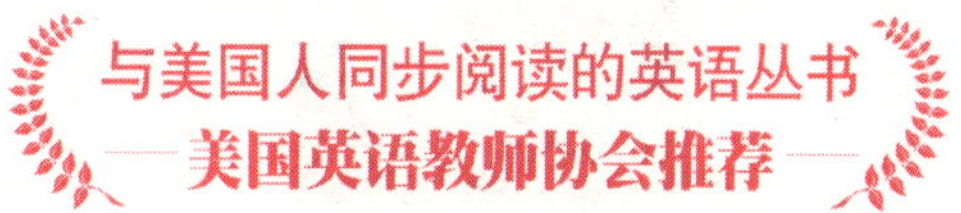

時代文藝出版社

图书在版编目（CIP）数据

那些年，那些诗：英汉对照／章华编译.—长春：时代文艺出版社，2009.11

（每天读一点英文）

ISBN 978-7-5387-2851-4

Ⅰ.那… Ⅱ.章… Ⅲ.①英语—汉语—对照读物

②诗歌—作品集—世界 Ⅳ.H319.4：I

中国版本图书馆CIP数据核字（2009）第211533号

出 品 人 张四季

策 划 人 博集天卷·辛 艳 刘宇圣

责任编辑 苗欣宇 付 娜

装帧设计 张丽娜 李 洁

那些年，那些诗

章 华 编译

出版发行／时代文艺出版社

地址／长春市泰来街1825号 时代文艺出版社 邮编／130062

总编办／0431-86012927 发行科／0431-86012939

网址／www.shidaichina.com

印刷／北京嘉业印刷厂

开本／880×1230毫米 1/32 字数／260千字 印张／10

版次／2009年12月第1版 印次／2010年2月第2次印刷 定价／23.80元

图书如有印装错误 请寄回印厂调换

目录

I Loved You 我曾经爱过你

Sadness of August
八月的忧愁

………… Goodbye Again，Cambridge …………

再别康桥

·········· I Love This Land ··········

我爱这土地

那些年，那些诗

Those days, those poems

Facing the Sea with Spring Blossoms

面朝大海，春暖花开

Facing the Sea with Spring Blossoms

Hai Zi

From tomorrow on,
I will be a happy man;
Grooming, chopping,
and traveling all over the world.

From tomorrow on,
I will care **foodstuff** and vegetable,
Living in a house towards the sea,
with spring blossoms.

From tomorrow on,
write to each of my dear ones,
Telling them of my happiness,
What the lightening of happiness has told me,
I will spread it to each of them.

Give a warm name for every river and every mountain,
Strangers, I will also wish you happy.
May you have a brilliant future!
*May you lovers **eventually** become spouses!*
May you enjoy happiness in this earthly world!
*I only wish to face the sea, with spring **blossoms**.*

面朝大海，春暖花开

海　子

从明天起，做一个幸福的人
喂马，劈柴，周游世界
从明天起，关心柴米油盐
我有一所房子，面朝大海，春暖花开。

从明天起，和每一个亲人通信
告诉他们我的幸福
那幸福的闪电告诉我的
我将告诉每一个人。

给每一条河每一座山取一个温暖的名字
陌生人，我也为你祝福
愿你有一个灿烂的前程
愿有情人终成眷属
愿你在尘世获得幸福
我只愿面朝大海，春暖花开。

实战提升
Practising & Exercise

背景知识

海子（1964-1989），原名查海生，1964 年 5 月出生在安徽省安庆城外的高河查湾。1979 年 15 岁时考入北京大学法律系，1982 年开始诗歌创作，1983 年毕业后任教于中国政法大学。1989 年 3 月 26 日，他在河北省山海关卧轨自杀。先后出版的诗集有《河流》、《传说》、《但是水、水》，另有长诗《土地》和仪式诗剧三部曲之一《弑》。

这首诗的开始时对“幸福”的渴望，以及“幸福”的所指，在诗中被不断地延宕和消解。生存和经验的封闭、局限状态，会助长现实虚空感；或者诗人只能将自己的存在悬系于形而上的层面上，和对于“幸福”的想象感受比较起来，诗人更多地感到来自内心追问和内心矛盾困惑的痛苦。思考的孤独感和焦虑感更为沉重实在，构成了海子诗歌的精神核心。

单词注解

foodstuff ['fu:dstʌf] 食料；粮食
eventually [i'ventjuəli] 最后，终于
blossom ['blɔsɔm] 开花；开花期

名句诵读

From tomorrow on，I will be a happy man；Grooming，chopping，and traveling all over the world.

Give a warm name for every river and every mountain，Strangers，I will also wish you happy. May you have a brilliant future! May you lovers eventually become spouses! May you enjoy happiness in this earthly world! I only wish to face the sea，with spring blossoms.

Sonnet 18

William Shakespeare

Shall I compare thee to a summer's day?
Thou **art** *more lovely and more temperate:*
Rough winds do shake the darling buds of May,
And summer's lease hath all too short a date:
Sometime too hot the eye of heaven shines
And often is his gold **complexion** dimmed;
And every fair from fair sometimes declines,
By chance or nature's changing course untrimmed:
But thy ***eternal*** *summer shall not* ***fade***, .
Nor lose possession of that fair thou ow'st.
Nor shall death **brag** thou wander'st in his shade,
When in eternal lines to time thou grow'st,
So long as men can breathe, or eyes can see,
So long lives this, and this gives life to thee.

第 18 号十四行诗

威廉 · 莎士比亚

我怎么能把你比作夏天呢?
你比它可爱也比它温婉:
狂风把五月的花蕾摇撼,
夏天的足迹匆匆而去:
天上的眼睛有时照得太炽烈,
它那炳耀的金颜又常遭掩蔽:
被机缘或无常的天道所摧折,
没有芳艳不凋残或不销毁。
但是你的长夏永远不会凋歇,
你的美艳亦不会遭到损失,
死神也力所不及,
当你在不朽的诗里与时同长。
只要一天有人类,或人有眼睛,
这诗将长存,并赐予你生命。

背景知识

威廉·莎士比亚（William Shakespeare），英国文艺复兴时期伟大的剧作家、诗人，欧洲文艺复兴时期人文主义文学的集大成者。他写过 154 首十四行诗，三或四首长诗。他是“英国戏剧之父”，本·琼斯称他为“时代的灵魂”，马克思称他为“人类最伟大的天才之一”，公认为“人类文学奥林匹斯山上的宙斯”。

这是莎士比亚 154 首十四行诗中的第 18 首。诗人将自己的心上人比作夏日的一天，又指出夏天其实没有那么完美，夏天不光短暂，还有狂风、骄阳和阴暗；诗人接着说任何美丽都会时过境迁，而只要这些诗篇流传，她就永远活在人们心间。

单词注解

art=are

complexion [kəm'plekʃən] 面色，肤色；气色

eternal [i(:)'tə:nl] 永久的，永恒的；无穷的

fade [feid] 凋谢，枯萎

brag [bræg] 吹牛，自吹

名句诵读

Shall I compare thee to a summer's day? Thou art more lovely and more temperate：

But thy eternal summer shall not fade，Nor lose possession of that fair thou ow'st.

So long as men can breathe，or eyes can see，So long lives this，and this gives life to thee.

沙　丘

罗伯特・弗洛斯特

海浪是绿色而潮湿的，
但从它们平息的处所，
依然卷着更大的浪涛，
而且是褐色的干燥的。

那是变成沙丘的海洋，
涌进渔夫栖息的村镇，
想用坚硬的沙子掩埋，
海水不能淹死的人们。

海或许了解海湾与海角，
却永远无法了解人类，
若她以为改变了形状，
就可以剪断人的思想。

人们留给了她一条船，使其沉没：
同样也能淹没一座小屋；
她们会更加自由地想着，
再一次抛弃那无用的外壳。

实战提升
Practising & Exercise

背景知识

罗伯特 · 弗洛斯特（Robert Frost），20 世纪美国最杰出的诗人，作品以朴素、深邃著称。他拥有四个普利策诗歌奖、44 种名誉学位和种种荣誉。他徒步漫游过许多地方，被认为是“新英格兰的农民诗人”。

在这首看似简单的诗歌里，诗人通过人和大海关系的思考来映射生与死，身体与思想之间的关系。

单词注解

dune [dju:n] 沙丘

cape [keip] 岬，海角

hut [hʌt] 小屋

shell [ʃel] 壳，贝壳

名句诵读

Sea waves are green and wet，But up from where they die，Rise others vaster yet，And those are brown and dry.

She may know cove and cape，But she does not know mankind
If by any change of shape，She hopes to cut off mind.

Men left her a ship to sink：They can leave her a hut as well；And be but more free to think For the one more cast-off shell.

Ode to the West Wind

Percy Bysshe Shelley

I

O wild West Wind, thou breath of Autumn's being,
Thou, from whose unseen presence the leaves dead
Are driven, like ghosts from an enchanter fleeing.

Yellow, and black, and pale, and hectic red,
Pestilence-stricken **multitudes**: O thou,
Who chariotest to their dark wintry bed

The winged seeds, where they lie cold and low,
Each like a corpse within its grave, until
Thine **azure** sister of the Spring shall blow

Her **clarion** o'er the dreaming earth, and fill
(Driving sweet buds like flocks to feed in air)
With living hues and odors plain and hill;

Wild Spirit, which art moving everywhere;
Destroyer and preserver; hear, O hear!

II

Thou on whose stream, 'mid the steep sky's commotion,
Loose clouds like earth's decaying leaves are shed,
Shook from the tangled boughs of Heaven and Ocean,

Angels of rain and lightning: there are spread
On the blue surface of thine aery surge,
Like the bright hair uplifted from the head

Of some fierce Maenad, even from the dim verge
Of the horizon to the zenith's height,
The locks of the approaching storm. Thou dirge

Of the dying year, to which this closing night
Will be the dome of a vast sepulchre,
Vaulted with all thy congregated might

Of vapours, from whose solid atmosphere
Black rain, and fire, and hail will burst: O hear!

III

Thou who didst waken from his summer dreams
The blue Mediterranean, where he lay,
Lulled by the coil of his crystalline streams,

Beside a pumice isle in Baiae's bay,
And saw in sleep old palaces and towers
Quivering within the wave's intenser day,

All overgrown with azure moss and flowers
So sweet，the sense faints picturing them!Thou
For whose path the Atlantic's level powers

Cleave themselves into chasms，while far below
The sea–blooms and the oozy woods which wear
The sapless foliage of the ocean，know

Thy voice，and suddenly grow gray with fear，
And tremble and despoil themselves：O hear!

Ⅳ

If I were a dead leaf thou mightest bear；
If I were a swift cloud to fly with thee；
A wave to pant beneath thy power，and share

The impulse of thy strength，only less free
Than thou，O uncontrollable! If even
I were as in my boyhood，and could be

The comrade of thy wanderings over Heaven，
As then，when to outstrip thy skiey speed
Scarce seemed a vision；I would ne'er have striven

As thus with thee in prayer in my sore need.
O，lift me as a wave，a leaf，a cloud!
I fall upon the thorns of life! I bleed!

A heavy weight of hours has chained and bowed

One too like thee： tameless，and swift，and proud.

V

Make me thy lyre，even as the forest is：
What if my leaves are falling like its own!
The tumult of thy mighty harmonies

Will take from both a deep，autumnal tone，
Sweet though in sadness. Be thou，Spirit fierce，
My spirit! Be thou me，impetuous one!

Drive my dead thoughts over the universe
Like withered leaves to quicken a new birth!
And，by the incantation of this verse，

Scatter，as from an unextinguished hearth
Ashes and sparks，my words among mankind!
Be through my lips to unawakened earth

The trumpet of a prophecy! O Wind,
If Winter comes，can Spring be far behind?

西风颂

珀西·比西·雪莱

一

哦，狂暴的西风啊，你是秋天的气息，
你神出鬼没，万木之叶因此皆枯，
黄叶乱窜，有如鬼魅碰到了巫师。

万叶乱飞，那颜色好似在躲避病魔，
枯黄、乌黑、苍白、潮红，
你啊，正驱使着长翅的种子赶赴到

黑暗、低矮、阴冷的床上过冬
每粒种子就像坟墓里的僵尸，
待到明媚的东君把号角吹响，

大地处处复苏，不再如梦迷离，
唤出嫩芽，像羊群一样，觅食空中
高山平原，姹紫嫣红，弥漫芳菲。

不羁的精灵呵，你无处不远行；
破坏者兼保护者：听吧，你且聆听！

二

没入你的急流，当高空一片混乱，
流云像大地的枯叶一样被撕扯
脱离天空和海洋的纠缠的枝干。

这是雨和电的先遣，
它们飘落在你的磅礴的、蔚蓝的波涛之上，
有如狂女那飘扬的头发在闪烁，

从天穹的最遥远而模糊的边沿
直抵九霄的中天，到处都在摇曳
欲来雷雨的卷发，对濒死的一年

你是岁之将尽的挽歌，而这密集的黑夜
将成为它广大墓陵的一座圆顶，
而你，凝聚所有水汽的力量把穹顶力挽，

那是你的浑然之气，从它会迸涌
黑色的雨，冰雹和火焰：哦，你听！

三

你把蓝色的地中海从夏梦中摇醒，
那地中海在澄澈的波浪上闲躺着，
被澄澈水流的回旋催眠入梦，

就在巴亚海湾的一个浮石岛边，

你梦见了古老的宫殿和楼阁
在飘摇的水波中掠影浮光。

那里长满了青苔，盛开着鲜花，
那芬芳真迷人欲醉！呵，为了给你
让一条路，大西洋的汹涌的浪波
把自己向两边劈开，而深在渊底
那水藻和绿色森林
虽然枝叶扶疏，却没有精力；

听到你的声音，它们已吓得发青：
一边颤栗，一边自动萎缩：哦，你听！

四

假如我是能被你唤起的一片枯叶，
假如我是能随你飞去的一片流云，
如果我是一个浪花在你的威力中喘息，

假如我能有你的脉搏，只是不像
你那么自由，哦，无法约束的生命！
假如我还在童年，能与你一道同行，

便成了你的伴侣，悠游天空
因为，那时候，要想追你上云霄，
似乎并非梦幻，我就不致像如今

这样焦躁地要和你争相祈祷。

哦，举起我吧，当我是水波、树叶、浮云！
我跌在生活的荆棘上，我流血了！

这被岁月的重轭所制服的生命
原是和你一样：所向空阔，自由自在，无拘无束。

五

把我当作弦琴吧，有如树林：
尽管我的叶落了，但又有何妨！
你巨大的合奏所振起的音乐

将染有树林和我的深邃的秋意：
虽忧伤而甜蜜。呵，但愿你给予我
狂暴的精神！愿你化为我，势不可挡！

请把我枯死的思想向世界吹落，
让它像枯叶一样促成新的生命！
尽这首诗的魔力之所能，

就把我的话语，像是灰烬和火种
在还未熄灭的炉火向人间播散！
通过我的口把预言的号角吹响，

去唤醒沉睡的大地吧！西风你听我说：
如果冬天已经来临，春天还会远吗？

背景知识

珀西·比西·雪莱(Percy Bysshe Shelley),19世纪英国著名浪漫主义诗人。是英国文学史上最有才华的抒情诗人之一,被誉为“诗人中的诗人”。其一生见识广阔,不仅是柏拉图主义者,更是个伟大的理想主义者。他创作的诗歌节奏明快,积极向上。

这首诗可以说是诗人“骄傲、轻捷而不驯的灵魂”的自白,是时代精神的写照。诗人凭借自己的诗才,借助自然的精灵让自己的生命与鼓荡的西风相呼相应,以饱含激情的笔触抒写了“秋的呼吸——奔放的西风”,创造了既是破坏者又是保护者的西风形象。感情真挚磅礴,格调高昂激越,用气势恢宏的篇章唱出了生命的旋律和心灵的狂舞。

单词注解

multitude ['mʌltitju:d] 许多
azure ['æʒə] 天蓝色的,蔚蓝的
clarion ['klæriən] 号角
aery ['e:ri] 梦幻般的,飘渺的
verge [və:dʒ] 边际,界限

名句诵读

O wild West Wind, thou breath of Autumn's being, Thou, from whose unseen presence the leaves dead Are driven, like ghosts from an enchanter fleeing.

Wild Spirit, which art moving everywhere; Destroyer and preserver; hear, O hear!

The trumpet of a prophecy! O Wind, If Winter comes, can Spring be far behind?

Sand Dunes

Robert Frost

Sea waves are green and wet,
But up from where they die,
Rise others vaster yet,
And those are brown and dry.

They are the sea made land
To come at the fisher town,
And bury in solid sand
The men she could not drown.

She may know cove and ***cape****,*
But she does not know mankind
If by any change of shape,
She hopes to cut off mind.

Men left her a ship to sink:
They can leave her a ***hut*** *as well;*
And be but more free to think
For the one more cast-off ***shell****.*

Homesick

Yu Guangzhong

When I was a child, my homesickness was a small stmap
Linking Mum at the other end and me this.

When I grown up, I remained **homesick**, but it became a ticket.
By which I sailed to and from my bride at the other end.

Then homesickness took the ***shape*** *of the grave,*
Mum inside of it and me outside.

Now I'm still homesick, but it is a narrow ***strait***
Separating *me on this side and the mainland on the other.*

乡　愁

余光中

小时候
乡愁是一枚小小的邮票
我在这头
母亲在那头

长大后
乡愁是一张窄窄的船票
我在这头
新娘在那头

后来啊
乡愁是一方矮矮的坟墓
我在外头
母亲在里头

而现在
乡愁是一湾浅浅的海峡
我在这头
大陆在那头

背景知识

余光中（1928- ），祖籍福建永春，生于江苏南京，当代著名诗人和评论家。1946 年考入厦门大学外文系。1947 年入金陵大学外语系（后转入厦门大学），1948 年发表第一首诗作，1949 年随父母迁香港，次年赴台，就读于台湾大学外文系。1953 年，与覃子豪、钟鼎文等共创"蓝星"诗社。后赴美进修，获美国爱荷华大学艺术硕士学位。已出版的诗集有《蓝色的羽毛》、《钟乳石》、《莲的联想》、《五陵少年》、《天国夜市》、《白玉苦瓜》、《隔水观音》等。

诗人的思乡之愁不是直白地说出来的，而是通过联想、想象，塑造了四幅生活艺术形象（邮票、船票、坟墓、海峡），使之呈现在读者眼前。作者把对母亲、妻子、祖国的思念、眷念之情熔于一炉，表达出渴望亲人团聚、国家统一的强烈愿望。

单词注解

homesick ['həumsik] 思家的

shape [ʃeip] 形状；样子

strait [streit] 海峡

separate ['sepəreit] 分隔；分割

名句诵读

When I was a child，my homesickness was a small stmap Linking Mum at the other end and me this.

Then homesickness took the shape of the grave，Mum inside of it and me outside.

Now I'm still homesick，but it is a narrow strait Separating me on this side and the mainland on the other.

Believe in the Future

Shi Zhi

When **cobwebs** *relentlessly clog my stove*
When its dying smoke sighs for poverty
I will stubbornly dig out the disappointing ash
And write with beautiful snowflakes: Believe in the Future

When my overripe grapes melt into late autumn **dew**
When my fresh flower lies in another's arms
I will stubbornly write on the bleak earth
With a dry frozen vine: Believe in the Future

I point to the waves billowing in the distance
I want to be the sea that holds the sun in its palm
Take hold of the beautiful warm pen of the dawn
And write with a child-like hand: Believe in the Future

The reason why I believe so resolutely in the future is:
I believe in the eyes of the future's people
Their eyelashes that can brush away the ash of history
Their pupils that can see through the texts of time

It doesn't matter whether people shed contrite tears
For our rotten flesh, or our hesitancy, or the bitterness of our failure
Whether they view us with sneers or deep-felt sympathy
Or scornful smiles or pungent satire

I firmly believe that people will judge our spines
And our endless explorations, losses, failures and successes
With an enthusiastic, objective and fair evaluation
Yes, I await their judgement anxiously

Friends, please let us believe in the future
Believe in our unbending striving
Believe in our youth that can conquer *death*
Believe in the Future: believe in Life.

相信未来

食　指

当蜘蛛网无情地查封了我的炉台
当灰烬的余烟叹息着贫困的悲哀
我依然固执地铺平失望的灰烬
用美丽的雪花写下：相信未来

当我的紫葡萄化为深秋的露水
当我的鲜花依偎在别人的情怀
我依然固执地用凝霜的枯藤
在凄凉的大地上写下：相信未来

我要用手指那涌向天边的排浪
我要用手掌那托住太阳的大海
摇曳着曙光那枝温暖漂亮的笔杆
用孩子的笔体写下：相信未来

我之所以坚定地相信未来
是我相信未来人们的眼睛
她有拨开历史风尘的睫毛

她有看透岁月篇章的瞳孔

不管人们对于我们腐烂的皮肉
那些迷途的惆怅、失败的苦痛
是寄予感动的热泪、深切的同情
还是给以轻蔑的微笑、辛辣的嘲讽

我坚信人们对于我们的脊骨
那无数次的探索、迷途、失败和成功
一定会给予热情、客观、公正的评定
是的，我焦急地等待着他们的评定

朋友，坚定地相信未来吧
相信不屈不挠的努力
相信战胜死亡的年轻
相信未来、热爱生命。

背景知识

食指（1948- ），原名郭路生，被称为新诗潮诗歌第一人。20岁时写的名作《相信未来》、《海洋三部曲》、《这是四点零八分的北京》等以手抄本的形式在社会上广为流传。出版的诗集有《相信未来》、《食指 · 黑大春现代抒情诗合集》、《诗探索金库 · 食指卷》。

这首诗构思巧妙。前三节写我是怎样“相信未来”的，后三节写为什么要“相信未来”，最后一节呼唤人们带着对未来的信念去努力，去热爱，去生活。用语质朴，而思想深刻；性格鲜明，又令人折服。全诗以语言的时间艺术，与中国画式的空间艺术相结合，实现了诗人所反复讲述的“我的诗是一面窗户，是窗含西岭千秋雪”的艺术。通读该诗，虽然我们感受更多的是压抑是痛苦，但从诗人那压抑和痛苦的吟哦中，读者能真切地感受到诗人那撼人心魄的信念——无时不在渴望和憧憬着光明的未来，并为理想和光明而奋斗挣扎着。

单词注解

cobweb ['kɔbweb] 蜘蛛网；蜘蛛丝
dew [dju:] 露，露水
conquer ['kɔŋkə] 战胜；克服

名句诵读

When cobwebs relentlessly clog my stove When its dying smoke sighs for poverty I will stubbornly dig out the disappointing ash And write with beautiful snowflakes：Believe in the Future

The reason why I believe so resolutely in the future is：I believe in the eyes of the future's people Their eyelashes that can brush away the ash of history Their pupils that can see through the texts of time

Friends，please let us believe in the future Believe in our unbending striving Believe in our youth that can conquer death Believe in the Future：believe in Life.

Paradise Lost

John Milton

Nine times the space that measures day and night
To mortal men, he with his horrid crew
Lay **vanquished**, *rolling in the fiery gulf*
Confounded though immortal. But his doom
Reserved him to more wrath; for now the thought
Both of lost happiness and lasting pain
Torments him; round he throws his baleful eyes,
That witnessed huge affliction and dismay,
Mixed with obdurate pride and steadfast hate.
At once, as far as angels **ken**, *he views*
The dismal situation waste and wild.
A dungeon horrible, on all sides round
As one great **furnace** flamed; yet from those flames
No light, but rather darkness visible
Served only to discover sights of woe,
Regions of sorrow, doleful shades, where peace
And rest can never dwell, hope never comes
That comes to all, but torture without end
Still urges, and a fiery deluge, fed
With ever-burning sulphur unconsumed:

Such place Eternal Justice had prepared
For those rebellious; here their prison ordained
In utter darkness and their portion set
As far removed from God and light of Heaven
As from the centre thrice to th'utmost pole.
O how unlike the place from whence they fell!
There the companions of his fall, o'erwhelmed
With floods and whirlwinds of tempestuous fire,
He soon discerns; and, weltering by his side,
One next himself in power, and next in crime,
Long after known in Palestine, and named
Beelzebub. To whom th'arch-enemy,
And thence in Heaven called Satan, with bold words
Breaking the horrid silence thus began:
"If thou beest he but O how fallen! how changed
From him who in the happy realms of light
Clothed with transcendent brightness didst outshine
Myriads, though bright! if he whom mutual league,
United thoughts and counsels, equal hope
And hazard in the glorious enterprise,
Joined with me once, now misery hath joined
In equal ruin; into what pit thou seest
From what height fallen, so much the stronger proved
He with his thunder: and till then who knew
The force of those dire arms? Yet not for those,
Nor what the potent Victor in his rage
Can else inflict, do I repent or change,
Though changed in outward luster, that fixed mind
And high disdain, from sense of injured merit,

That with the Mightiest raised me to contend,
And to the fierce contention brought along
Innumerable force of spirits armed,
That durst dislike his reign, and me preferring,
His utmost power with adverse power opposed
In dubious battle on the plains of Heaven,
And shook his throne. What though tile field be lost?
All is not lost: the unconquerable will,
And study of revenge, immortal hate,
And courage never to submit or yield:
And what is else not to be overcome?
That glory never shall his wrath or might
Extort from me. To bow and sue for grace
With suppliant knee, and deify his power
Who from the terror of this arm so late
Doubted his empire that were low indeed;
That were an ignominy and shame beneath
This downfall; since by fate the strength of gods
And this empyreal substance cannot fail;
Since, through experience of this great event,
In arms not worse, in foresight much advanced,
We may with more successful hope resolve
To wage by force or guile eternal war,
Irreconcilable to our grand Foe,
Who now triumphs, and in th'excess of joy
Sole reigning holds the tyranny of Heaven."
So spake th' apostate angel, though in pain,
Vaunting aloud, but racked with deep despair.

…

失乐园节选

约翰·弥尔顿

根据人间的计算，大约九天九夜，
他和他那一伙可怕的徒众，
沉沦辗转在烈火的深渊中。
虽属不死之身，却与死者无异；
但这个刑罚反激起他更大的愤怒，
既失去了幸福，又饱受无穷痛苦的折磨。
当他抬起忧虑的双眼，环视周遭，
摆在眼前的是莫大的隐忧和烦恼，
交织着顽固的傲气和难消的憎恨。
霎时间，他竭尽天使的目力，
望断际涯，但见悲风弥漫，浩渺无垠，
可怕的地牢从四面八方圈着他，
像一个洪炉的烈火四射，但那火焰
却不发光，只是灰蒙蒙的一片，
但能辨认出那儿的苦难情景，
悲惨的境地和凄怆的暗影。
和平和安息绝不在那儿停留，
希望无所不到，唯独不到那里。

只有无穷无尽的苦难步步相跟
永燃的硫璜不断地添注，
不灭的火焰，洪水般向他们滚滚逼来。
这个地方，就是正义之神为那些
叛逆者准备的，在天外的冥荒中
为他们设置的牢狱，那个地方
远离天神和天界的亮光，
相当于天极到中心的三倍那么远。
啊，这里和他所从坠落的地方
简直有天壤之别呀！
和他一起坠落的伙伴们
淹没在烈火的洪流和旋风之中，
他依稀可辨，在他近旁挣扎的，
论权力和罪行都仅次于他的神魔，
后来在巴勒斯坦知道他的名字叫别西卜。
这个在天上叫做撒旦的首要神敌
以豪壮的言语打破可怕的沉寂，开始向他的伙伴这样说道：
“是你啊；这是何等的坠落！
何等的变化呀！你原来住在光明的乐土，
全身披覆着无比的光辉，
胜过群星的灿烂：
你曾和我结成同盟，同心敌忾，
搏击于光荣的大事业中
现在，我们是从高高在上的天界
沉沦到了不可测的深渊呀！他握有雷霆，
确是强大，谁知道这凶恶的

武器竟有那么大的威力呢?

可是，那威力，那强有力的

胜利者的狂暴，都不能

叫我沮丧，或者叫我改变初衷，

虽然外表的光环消失了，

但坚定的心志和岸然的骄矜

决不转变；由于真价的受损，

激动了我，决心和强权决一胜负，

率领无数天军投入剧烈的战斗，

他们都厌恶天神的统治而来拥护我，

拿出全部力量跟至高的权力对抗，

在天界疆上做一次冒险的战斗，

动摇了他的宝座。我们损失了什么?

并非一无所剩：坚定的意志、

热切的复仇心、不来的憎恨，

以及永不屈服、永不退让的勇气，

还有什么比这些更难战胜的吗?

他的暴怒也罢，威力也罢，

绝不能夺去我这份光荣。

经过这一次惨烈的战争，

好容易才使他的政权动摇；

这时还要卑躬屈膝，

向他哀求怜悯，拜倒在他的权力之下，

那才真正是卑鄙、可耻，

比这次的沉沦还要卑贱。

因为我们具有与生俱来的神力，

赋有轻清的灵质，不能朽坏，
又因这次大事件的教训，
我们要准备更好的武器，
更远的预见，更有成功的希望，
以暴力或智力向我们的大敌
挑起不可调解的持久战争。
他现在正沉湎于成功，得意忘形，
独揽大权，在天上掌握虐政呢。”
背叛的天使忍痛说出豪言壮语
心却为深沉的失望所苦。
……

实战提升
Practising & Exercise

背景知识

约翰 · 弥尔顿 (John Milton)，生于伦敦一个富裕的清教徒家庭，在剑桥大学求学时和毕业后一个时期，钻研古代和文艺复兴时期文学，深受人文主义思想熏陶。1638 年他旅行意大利，访问过被天主教会关在狱里的伽利略，并和意大利的文人学者交往。1639 年，英国革命形势紧张，他回国参加反对国王和国教的斗争。他因积劳过度，双目失明，但仍坚持斗争。王朝复辟后，他受到迫害，著作被焚毁，生活极其贫困。就在这个时期，他完成了三部杰作：《失乐园》、《复乐园》和《力士参孙》。

《失乐园》以史诗一般的磅礴气势揭示了人的原罪与堕落。诗中叛逆之神撒旦，因为反抗上帝的权威被打入地狱，却毫不屈服，为复仇寻至伊甸园。亚当与夏娃受被撒旦附身的蛇的引诱，偷吃了上帝明令禁吃的知识树上的果子。最终，撒旦及其同伙遭谴全变成了蛇，亚当与夏娃被逐出了伊甸园。该诗体现了诗人追求自由的崇高精神，是世界文学史、思想史上的一部极重要的作品！

单词注解

vanquish ['væŋkwiʃ] 征服，击败

ken [ken] 视野，眼界

furnace ['fəːnis] 火炉，熔炉

fierce [fiəs] 凶猛的；残酷的

empyreal [ˌempai'riːəl] 最高天的；太空的

名句诵读

Nine times the space that measures day and night To mortal men, he with his horrid crew Lay vanquished, rolling in the fiery gulf Confounded though immortal.

At once, as far as angels ken, he views The dismal situation waste and wild.

So spake th'apostate angel, though in pain, Vaunting aloud, but racked with deep despair.

The Chimney Sweeper

William Blake

When my mother died I was very young,
And my father sold me while yet my **tongue**
Could scarcely cry "'weep! weep! weep! weep!"
So your chimney I sweep, & in soot I sleep.

There's little Tom Dacre who cried when his head
That curl'd like a lamb's back, was shav'd, so I said,
"Hush, Tom! never mind it, for when our head's bare,
You know that the soot cannot **spoil** your white hair."

And so he was quiet, & that very night,
As Tom was a-sleeping he had such a sight!
That thousands of sweepers, Dick, Joe, Ned, & Jack,
Were all of them lock'd up in coffins of black;

And by came an angel who had a bright key,
And he open'd the **coffins** *& set them all free;*
Then down a green plain, leaping, laughing they run
And wash in a river, and shine in the sun;

Then naked & white，all their bags left behind，
They rise upon clouds，and sport in the wind，
And the angel told Tom，if he'd be a good boy，
He'd have God for his father，and never want joy.

And so Tom awoke；and we rose in the dark，
And got with our bags & our brushes to work.
Tho' the morning was cold，Tom was happy & warm；
So if all do their duty，they need not fear harm.

扫烟囱的小男孩

威廉·布莱克

我母亲死的时候，我还小，
我父亲把我卖给了别人，
我当时还不太喊得清“扫呀，扫呀，”
就这样白天扫你们的烟囱，晚上在烟灰里睡觉。

有个小汤姆，头发卷得像羊毛，
剃光的时候，哭得好伤心，好难受，
我就说：“小汤姆，别哭，光了头，
烟灰就不会糟蹋你的头发了。”

他平静了下来，当天夜里，
汤姆睡着了，梦见了这样的景象，
迪克，乔，南德，杰克等千千万万个扫烟囱小孩
统统被锁进了黑棺材。

后来来了个天使，拿了把金钥匙，
他打开棺材放出了孩子们（真是好天使！）
他们又跳又笑地来到了草地上，

洗浴于河水，晾晒于阳光。

把工具袋丢下，赤条条的，白白的，
他们升到云端，在风中嬉戏；
“只要你做个好孩子，”天使对汤姆说，
“上帝会做你的父亲，永不缺少欢喜。”

汤姆于是梦醒，我们在黑暗中起床，
拿起工具袋和刷子去干活。
晨风虽冷，汤姆自感心欢温暖；
如果所有人都恪尽职守，就不怕灾难。

背景知识

威廉 · 布莱克（William Blake），18 世纪末 19 世纪初英国著名的画家，英国文学史上最复杂、最有个性的诗人之一。布莱克的早期诗歌以颂扬爱情、向往欢乐与和谐为主题。他的诗歌语言质朴，形象鲜明，富有音乐感，充满瑰丽的想象和奔放的激情。后期诗作明显具有神秘主义倾向和宗教色彩，用象征的手法来表达深邃的思想。布莱克生活清贫，靠绘画和雕刻为生，他那富有个人灵念与想象力的恢弘诗篇生前并没有得到承认。英国文学界直到 19 世纪末才开始意识到他们原来忽略的的不仅仅是一位颇有造诣的版画家，而且还是一位诗哲。

在很多年以前，男孩们经常去扫烟囱。他们得爬到烟囱里面，刮干净煤烟，然后把它们扫走，这可是一项艰苦的工作，而且对身体非常有害。这首诗选自《天真之歌》，进一步表明“天真”是超越官能的感官束缚的关键，这样就赋予天真以深刻的内涵。

单词注解

tongue [tʌŋ] 说话能力；口才

spoil [spɔil] 损坏；糟蹋

coffin ['kɔfin] 棺材，灵柩

名句诵读

When my mother died I was very young，And my father sold me while yet my tongue Could scarcely cry “‘weep! weep! weep! weep!” So your chimney I sweep，& in soot I sleep.

And by came an angel who had a bright key，And he open'd the coffins & set them all free；Then down a green plain，leaping，laughing they run And wash in a river，and shine in the sun；

And so Tom awoke；and we rose in the dark，And got with our bags & our brushes to work. Tho'the morning was cold，Tom was happy & warm；So if all do their duty，they need not fear harm.

O Captain! My Captain

Walt Whitman

O Captain! my Captain! our fearful trip is done;
The ship has weathered every rack, the prize we sought is won.
The port is near, the bells I hear, the people all **exulting**,
While follow eyes the steady keel, the vessel grim and daring;
But O heart! heart! heart!
O the bleeding drops of red,
Where on the deck my Captain lies,
Fallen cold and dead.

O Captain! my Captain! rise up and hear the bells;
Rise up—for you the flag is flung—for you the ***bugle*** *trills.*
For you bouquets and ribboned wreaths —for you the shores
a-crowding,
For you they call, the swaying mass, their eager faces turning;
Here Captain! dear father!
This arm beneath your head;
It is some dream that on the deck,
You've fallen cold and dead.

My Captain does not answer, his lips are **pale** and still;

My father does not feel my arm，he has no pulse nor will；
The ship is **anchored** safe and sound，its voyage closed and done；
From fearful trip the victor ship comes in with object won；
Exult，O shores，and ring，O bells!
But I with mournful **tread**，
Walk the deck my Captain lies，
Fallen cold and dead.

哦，船长，我的船长！

瓦尔特·惠特曼

哦，船长，我的船长！我们所畏惧的的航程已经终结，
我们的船渡过了各种险关，我们寻求的奖赏已经得到。
前方就是港口，钟声我已听见，听到了人们的欢呼，
目迎着我们的船从容返航，威严而且勇敢；
可是，心啊！心啊！心啊！
哦，殷红的血滴流泻，
在甲板上，我的船长倒下了，
他已倒下，已死去，已冷却。

哦，船长，我的船长！起来听听这钟声吧，
起来，——旌旗为你招展——号角为你长鸣。
为你，岸上挤满了人群——为你，无数花束、彩带、花环。
为你，熙攘的群众在呼唤，转动着多少殷切的脸。
这里，船长！亲爱的父亲！
你的头枕在我的手臂上吧！
这是甲板上的一场梦啊，
你已倒下，已死去，已冷却。

我们的船长不作回答，他的双唇惨白而僵硬，
我的父亲感觉不到我的手臂，他已没有脉搏、没有生命，
我们的船已安全抛锚定泊，航行已完成，已告终，
胜利的船从险恶的旅途归来，目的已经达到；
欢呼吧，哦，海岸！轰鸣，哦，钟声！
但是，我迈着悲恸的步伐，
在甲板上，那里躺着我的船长，
他已倒下，已死去，已冷却。

背景知识

瓦尔特 · 惠特曼(Walt Whitman)，美国历史上最伟大的诗人，他创作的《草叶集》代表着美国浪漫主义文学的高峰，是世界文学宝库中的精品。在《草叶集》中，他歌颂的对象都是处于社会下层的体力劳动者，如车夫、矿工和农人等，并对美国的前途充满了信心，是一位真正的民族诗人。

惠特曼的诗大气磅礴，激情奔放，起伏跌宕。这是诗人惠特曼为悼念林肯而写下的著名诗篇。诗人用航船战胜惊涛骇浪到达港口比喻林肯领导的南北战争的胜利结束，以领航的船长象征林肯总统的丰功伟绩，在万众欢腾之中，以一曲悲歌，赞颂一位伟大人物。

单词注解

exult [ig'zʌlt] 狂喜；欢欣鼓舞
bugle ['bju:gl] 军号，喇叭
pale [peil] 苍白的，灰白的
anchor ['æŋkə] 锚
tread [tred] 步行，走

名句诵读

O Captain! my Captain! our fearful trip is done；The ship has weathered every rack，the prize we sought is won.

O Captain! my Captain! rise up and hear the bells；Rise up—for you the flag is flung—for you the bugle trills.

It is some dream that on the deck，You've fallen cold and dead.

I'm Nobody

Emily Dickinson

I'm nobody! Who are you?
Are you nobody, too?
Then there's a pair of us—don't tell!
They'd ***banish*** *us, you know.*

How ***dreary*** *to be somebody!*
How public, like a frog
To tell your name the livelong day
To an admiring ***bog****!*

我是无名之辈！

艾米莉·狄金森

我是无名之辈！你是谁？
你也是无名之辈？
那咱俩就成了一对——别出声！
他们会排挤咱们——要小心！
做个大人物多没劲！
多招摇——像只青蛙
对着欣赏的小水洼
整日里炫耀自己的名号！

实战提升
Practising & Exercise

背景知识

艾米莉 · 狄金森 (Emily Dickinson) 是美国 19 世纪诗歌史上重要的诗人，也是 20 世纪英美意象派诗歌的先驱。她虽然居住在新英格兰一个偏僻小镇里，足不出户、与世隔绝，然而她生活在自己的世界里，那是灵魂的世界，她的特殊使命就是表现那个世界。她以美玉般的诗歌完成了这一使命，使她成为前无古人后无来者的最伟大的美国女诗人。她在美国文学史中之所以占有重要地位，不是取决于她的诗歌的思想内容，而是取决于她的诗歌的技巧和形式。其怪诞的风格、奇特的意象、巧妙的暗喻和不拘形式的格局，成为西方近代和当代诗歌的一个重要渊源。狄金森与自然为伍，视自然为朋友。

狄金森对诗歌的传统规范表现了不驯的叛逆姿态。狄金森倾向于微观、内省，艺术气质近乎“婉约”。　她的语言，一洗铅华、不事雕饰、质朴清新，有一种“粗糙美”，有时又如小儿学语般幼稚。在韵律方面，她基本上采用四行一节、抑扬格四音步与三音步相间，偶数行押脚韵的赞美诗体。

单词注解

banish ['bæniʃ] 流放，放逐

dreary ['driəri] 沉闷的，阴郁的

bog [bɔg] 沼泽，泥塘

名句诵读

I'm nobody! Who are you? Are you nobody, too? Then there's a pair of us—don't tell! They'd banish us, you know.

How dreary to be somebody! How public, like a frog To tell your name the livelong day To an admiring bog!

Success

Emily Dickinson

Success is counted sweetest
By those who ne'er succeed.
To comprehend a nectar
Requires sorest need.

Not one of all the **purple** *host*
Who took the flag today
Can tell the definition
So clear, of **victory**,

As he, defeated, dying,
On—whose forbidden ear
The distant strains of **triumph**
Break, agonized and clear.

成 功

艾米莉·狄金森

从未成功的人认为，
成功的滋味甜美无比。
必须要有强烈的需求，
方能领会花蜜的美味。

那最显赫的人身着紫衣，
执掌今日的大旗，
似乎没有人能像他们那样，
明了胜利的真谛。

当他战败后垂死，
失聪的耳边突然响起
遥远的凯歌旋律
竟如此痛苦而清晰。

背景知识

艾米莉 · 狄金森 (Emily Dickinson)，现在被公认为是美国最优秀的诗人之一，可在她有生之年所发表的诗作却寥寥无几。她在马萨诸塞州的阿默斯特过着与世隔绝的生活。她生在家里，死在家里，尽管艾米莉 · 狄金森缺少社会阅历，但她却有丰富的内心世界，其诗歌的主题主要集中在爱情、死亡和自然这些永恒的主题上。

单词注解

purple ['pə:pl] 紫的，帝王的
victory ['viktəri] 胜利；战胜
triumph ['traiəmf] 成功，业绩

名句诵读

Success is counted sweetest By those who ne'er succeed.

Not one of all the purple host Who took the flag today Can tell the definition So clear，of victory，

As he，defeated，dying，On—whose forbidden ear The distant strains of triumph Break，agonized and clear.

O Solitude!

John Keats

*O Solitude! if I must with thee **dwell**,*
Let it not be among the jumbled heap
Of murky buildings; climb with me the steep,
Nature's observatory—whence the dell,
*Its flowery **slopes**, its river's crystal swell.*
May seem a span; let me thy vigils keep
'Mongst boughs pavillion'd, where the deer's swift leap
Startles the wild bee from the fox-glove bell.
But though I'll gladly trace these scenes with thee,
*Yet the sweet **converse** of an innocent mind,*
Whose words are images of thoughts refin'd,
Is my soul's pleasure; and it sure must be
*Almost the highest **bliss** of human-kind,*
*When to thy haunts two kindred spirits **flee**.*

哦，孤独

约翰·济慈

哦，孤独！假若我和你必须
同住，可别在这层叠的一片
灰色建筑里，让我们爬上山，
到大自然的观测台去，从那里——
山谷、晶亮的河，锦簇的草坡
看来只是一拃；让我守着你
在枝叶荫蔽下，看跳纵的鹿麇
把指顶花盅里的蜜蜂惊吓。
不过，虽然我喜欢和你赏玩
这些景色，我的心灵更乐于
和纯洁的心灵亲切会谈；
她的言语是优美情思的表象
因为我相信，人的至高的乐趣
是一对心灵避入你的港湾。

实战提升
Practising & Exercise

背景知识

约翰 · 济慈（John Keats），英国浪漫主义著名诗人。济慈诗才横溢，与雪莱、拜伦齐名。他的生命只有 25 年，可他的诗篇一直誉满人间，被认为完美地体现了西方浪漫主义诗歌的特色，并被推崇为欧洲浪漫主义运动的杰出代表。济慈一生饱经孤独的煎熬，为此，他特别喜爱和亲近自然万物，特别憧憬理想的爱情，并选择了诗歌创作作为自我存在的基本方式。分析和把握济慈的孤独体验对于我们理解济慈其人及其诗歌创作具有重要的意义。

单词注解

dwell [dwel] 居住，住
slope [sləup] 坡；斜面
converse [kən'və:s]【书】交谈，谈话
bliss [blis] 天赐之福，福气
flee [fli:] 消失；消散

名句诵读

O Solitude! if I must with thee dwell, Let it not be among the jumbled heap Of murky buildings; climb with me the steep, Nature's observatory—whence the dell, Its flowery slopes, its river's crystal swell.

But though I'll gladly trace these scenes with thee, Yet the sweet converse of an innocent mind, Whose words are images of thoughts refin'd, Is my soul's pleasure; and it sure must be Almost the highest bliss of human-kind, When to thy haunts two kindred spirits flee.

I've Been Working on the Railroad

I've been working on the railroad,

All the live-long day.

I've been working on the railroad,

Just to pass the time away.

Can't you hear the **whistle** *blowing,*

Rise up so early in the morn;

Can't you hear the captain shouting,

"Dinah, blow your **horn**!"

Dinah, won't you blow?

Dinah, won't you blow?

Dinah, won't you blow your horn?

Dinah, won't you blow?

Dinah, won't you blow?

Dinah, won't you blow your horn?

Someone's in the kitchen with Dinah,

Someone's in the kitchen I know,

Someone's in the kitchen with Dinah,

Strummin'on the old banjo, and singin'

Fee-fi-fidd-lee-i-o,

Fee-fi-fidd-lee-i-o,

Fee-fi-fidd-lee-i-o,

Strummin'on the old **banjo**.

我一直工作在铁道上

我一直工作在铁道上，
整天从早干到晚。
我一直工作在铁道上，
只是为了消磨时光。
难道你没听见哨声响？
清晨一大早就得起身；
难道你没听见队长叫？
“黛娜，快吹响你的号！”

黛娜，你别吹，
黛娜，你别吹，
黛娜，你别吹号。
黛娜，你别吹，
黛娜，你别吹，
黛娜，你别吹号。
有人同黛娜在伙房，
我知道有人在伙房。
有人同黛娜在伙房，
拨响老班卓在歌唱：
菲——费费德——利——伊——哟，
菲——费费德——利——伊——哟，
拨响老班卓。

背景知识

《我一直工作在铁道上》是最流行的美国民歌之一。它最早是十九世纪三四十年代路易斯安娜州密西西比河南部修筑河堤的黑人工人们唱的《大堤曲》。随着筑大堤变为建铁路，这强有力的曲调被填上新词，成了密西西比州西部大多数爱尔兰铁路工人唱的一支歌。到 1880 年为止，各民族以及来自各国的工人们已经铺设了近十万英里的铁道，《我一直工作在铁道上》这支歌也已经传遍了 38 个州。这首歌的另一翻版《得克萨斯州的眼睛》被得克萨斯州大学用作正式校歌。其中以“黛娜，你别吹”开始的第二段是后来加进去的。以前各大学经常刊印歌本，而《我一直工作在铁道上》这首歌总是名列其中。

单词注解

whistle ['hwisl] 口哨；警笛；哨子
horn [hɔ:n] 触角，触须
banjo ['bændʒəu] 五弦琴

名句诵读

I've been working on the railroad，All the live-long day.

Can't you hear the whistle blowing，Rise up so early in the morn；
Can't you hear the captain shouting，“Dinah，blow your horn!”

…………I Loved You…………

我曾经爱过你

The Furthest Distance in the World

Rabindranath Tagore

The furthest distance in the world is
not between life and death
But when I stand in front of you
Yet you don't know that I love you

The furthest distance in the world is
not when I stand in front of you
Yet you can't see my love
But when ***undoubtedly*** *knowing the love from both*
Yet cannot be together

The furthest distance in the world is
not being apart while being in love
But when **plainly** can not **resist** the yearning
Yet pretending you have never been in my heart

The furthest distance in the world is
not when plainly can not resist the yearning
Yet pretending you have never been in my heart
But using one's indifferent heart
to dig an uncrossable river for the one who loves you

世界上最遥远的距离

罗宾德拉纳特 · 泰戈尔

世界上最遥远的距离
不是生与死
而是我就站在你的面前
你却不知道我爱你

世界上最遥远的距离
不是我站在你面前
你却不知道我爱你
而是明明知道彼此相爱
却不能在一起

世界上最遥远的距离
不是明明知道彼此相爱
却不能在一起
而是明明无法抵挡这股想念
却还得故意装作丝毫没有把你放在心里

世界上最遥远的距离

不是明明无法抵挡这股想念

却还得故意装作丝毫没有把你放在心里

而是用自己冷漠的心

为爱你的人挖掘了一条无法跨越的沟渠

背景知识

罗宾德拉纳特 · 泰戈尔 (Rabindranath Tagore), 印度著名诗人、作家、艺术家、社会活动家、哲学家和印度民族主义者，生于加尔各答市一个有深厚文化教养的家庭，属于婆罗门种姓。1913 年他凭借宗教抒情诗《吉檀迦利》获得诺贝尔文学奖。

在这首诗歌中，作者阐述了：生与死本是一种永远无法逾越的距离，而近在咫尺却形同陌路是单恋的心与所爱的人之间遥远的距离。相爱却不能在一起，有情人无法成眷属，是千古遗憾的情人之间的距离，而明明爱着却装着不放在心上，是更加矛盾而痛苦的距离。

单词注解

undoubtedly [ʌn'dautidli] 毫无疑问地；肯定地
plainly ['pleinli] 清楚地，明显地
resist [ri'zist] 抵抗，反抗

名句诵读

The furthest distance in the world is not between life and death But when I stand in front of you Yet you don't know that I love you

The furthest distance in the world is not when I stand in front of you Yet you can't see my love But when undoubtedly knowing the love from both Yet cannot be together

The furthest distance in the world is not when plainly can not resist the yearning Yet pretending you have never been in my heart But using one's indifferent heart to dig an uncrossable river for the one who loves you

Ode to the Oak

Shu Ting

If I fall in love with you—
I will never resemble clambering **trumpet** creeper,
To flaunt myself by your high branches.

If I fall in love with you—
I will never imitate spoony birds,
To repeat simple songs for green shade.

I will not only resemble a wellspring,
To bring you cool consolation **perennially**;
I will not only resemble steepy mountains,
To increase your altitude or set off your dignified manner.

Even not only sunlight,
Even not only spring rain,
No, these are not enough!

*I must be a **kapok** beside you,*
As an image of tree I stand with you.
Our roots hold tightly in the earth,

Our leaves touch gently in the clouds.

As each breeze passes, we salute each other,
But no one can understand our own words.

You have your iron trunk and copper branch
Like a knife, a sword and a halberd as well;
I have my red and big flowers,
Like a heavy sigh and a **heroic** torch as well.

Together we partake cold waves, storms and firebolts;
Together we share fogs, flowing hazes and rainbows,
We seem always apart, but interdependent all life long.

Only this is great love,
Faithfulness lies here:
I love not only your ***gigantic*** *stature,*
But also the position you uphold,
And the earth on which you stand.

致橡树

舒　婷

我如果爱你——
绝不像攀缘的凌霄花，
借你的高枝炫耀自己；

我如果爱你——
绝不学痴情的鸟儿，
为绿荫重复单调的歌曲；

也不止像泉源，
常年送来清凉的慰籍；
也不止像险峰，
增加你的高度，衬托你的威仪。

甚至日光。
甚至春雨。
不，这些都还不够！

我必须是你近旁的一株木棉，

做为树的形象和你站在一起。
根，紧握在地下，
叶，相触在云里。

每一阵风过，
我们都互相致意，
但没有人
听懂我们的言语。

你有你的铜枝铁干，
像刀，像剑，
也像戟；
我有我的红硕花朵，
像沉重的叹息，
又像英勇的火炬。

我们分担寒潮、风雷、霹雳；
我们共享雾霭、流岚、虹霓，
仿佛永远分离，
却又终身相依。

这才是伟大的爱情，
坚贞就在这里：
不仅爱你伟岸的身躯，
也爱你坚持的位置，脚下的土地。

实战提升
Practising & Exercise

背景知识

舒婷，原名龚佩瑜，朦胧诗派代表诗人之一。1952 年出生于福建石码镇，1969 年下乡插队，1972 年返城当工人。1979 年开始发表诗歌作品。1980 年至福建省文联工作，从事专业写作。主要著作有诗集《双桅船》、《会唱歌的鸢尾花》、《始祖鸟》，散文集《心烟》等。

诗人以橡树为对象表达了爱情的热烈、诚挚和坚贞。诗中的橡树不是一个具体的对象，而是诗人理想中的情人象征。因此，这首诗一定程度上不是单纯倾诉自己的热烈爱情，而是要表达一种爱情的理想和信念，通过亲切具体的形象来发挥，颇有古人托物言志的意味。

单词注解

trumpet ['trʌmpit] 喇叭；小号
perennially [pə'renjəli] 永久地
kapok ['keipɔk] 木棉花，木丝棉
heroic [hi'rəuik] 英雄的，英勇的
gigantic [dʒai'gæntik] 巨人般的，巨大的

名句诵读

If I fall in love with you—I will never imitate spoony birds，To repeat simple songs for green shade.

I must be a kapok beside you，As an image of tree I stand with you.

Only this is great love，Faithfulness lies here：I love not only your gigantic stature，But also the position you uphold，And the earth on which you stand.

The Passionate Shepherd to His Love

Christopher Marlowe

Come live with me and be my love,
And we will all the pleasures prove.
That valleys, groves, hills, and fields,
Woods, or steepy mountain ***yields****.*

And we will sit upon the rocks,
Seeing the shepherds feed their flocks,
By shallow rivers to whose falls
Melodious birds sing **madrigals**.

And I will make thee beds of roses
And a thousand ***fragrant*** *posies,*
A cap of flowers, and a kirtle,
Embroidered all with leaves of myrtle;

A gown made of the finest wool
Which from our pretty lambs we pull;
Fair lined slippers for the cold,
With buckles of the purest gold;

A belt of straw and ivy buds,
With coral clasps and **amber** studs:
And if these pleasures may thee move,
Come live with me, and be my love.

The shepherds's wains shall dance and sing
For thy delight each May morning:
If these delights thy mind may move,
Then live with me and be my love.

激情的牧羊人致心爱的姑娘

克里斯托夫 · 马洛

来吧，和我生活在一起，做我的爱人，
在这里，我们将快乐无边，
这里有峻峭秀丽的山峦，
还有风光明媚的山谷田园。

在那边，我俩坐在山岩上，
看牧羊人喂养可爱的羔羊，
在浅浅的小溪旁，
鸟儿随着潺潺流水，唱着情歌。

在那边，我将用玫瑰编一顶花冠，
用成千的花束做床，
用爱神木的叶子织成长裙，
一切都献给你，绚丽与芬芳。

我从羔羊身上剪下最好的羊毛，
为你做防寒的鞋衬和长袍；
用纯金为你制作鞋扣，

该有多么珍贵，多么荣耀。

我用长春藤和芳草做腰带，
珊瑚带扣点缀着琥珀水晶。
假如这些享受能打动你的心，
来吧，和我生活在一起，做我的爱人。

只要你能快乐，五月的每天早上，
牧羊人都为你你纵情舞蹈，高歌入云，
如果这些欢乐能让你动情，
来吧，和我生活在一起，做我的爱人。

实战提升

Practising & Exercise

背景知识

克里斯托夫 · 马洛 (Christopher Marlowe)，英国诗人，剧作家。1564 年 3 月 6 日生于坎特伯雷一富有鞋匠之家，1593 年 5 月 30 日卒于伦敦附近的德特福德。被誉为“大学才子”的马洛革新了中世纪的戏剧，在舞台上创造了反映时代精神的巨人性格和“雄伟的诗行”，为莎士比亚的创作铺平了道路。

这首诗是英国文学诗中最优美的抒情诗。它继承了田园抒情诗的风格。诗中的牧羊人享受着乡村生活，酝酿着对爱人的纯洁感情。通过描写恋人们在无世事尘嚣干扰的山野怀抱中生活，传达了一段只可意会，不可言传的真情。

单词注解

yield [ji:ld] 出产；结出

madrigal ['mædrigəl] 情歌；小调

fragrant ['freigrənt] 香的，芳香的

amber ['æmbə] 琥珀

名句诵读

Come live with me and be my love, And we will all the pleasures prove. That valleys, groves, hills, and fields, Woods, or steepy mountain yields.

And I will make thee beds of roses And a thousand fragrant posies, A cap of flowers, and a kirtle, Embroidered all with leaves of myrtle;

The shepherds's wains shall dance and sing For thy delight each May morning: If these delights thy mind may move, Then live with me and be my love.

When We Two Parted

George Gordon Byron

When we two parted
In silence and tears,
Half broken–hearted
To serve for years,
Pale grew thy *cheek and cold,*
Colder thy kiss,
Truly that hour foretold
Sorrow to this!

The dew of the morning
Suck chill *or my brow*
It felt like the warning
Of what I feel now.
Thy cows are all broken,
And light is thy fame;
I hear thy name spoken,
And share in its shame.

They name thee before me,
A knell to mine ear;

A shudder comes o'er me
Why wert thou so dear?
Thy know not I knew thee,
who knew thee too well:
Long, Long shall I rue thee
Too deeply to tell.

In secret we met–
In silence I grieve
That thy heart could forget,
Thy spirit deceive.
If I should meet thee
After long years,
How should I greet thee?
With silence and tears.

我们俩分别时

乔治·戈登·拜伦

我们俩分别时
相对无言地垂泪
两颗心一半裂碎，
因为即将多年相违，
你的面容苍白冰冷，
更冷的是你的吻；
那时刻真的预兆着
今日的伤心。

那天清晨的寒露
冷彻了我的眉宇—
它像是告诫
我今日的感触。
你背弃山盟海誓
名声变得轻浮：
我听别人提起你的姓名，
我就会感到羞辱。

人们在我面前提起你，

我听来犹如丧钟；

我忍不住周身颤栗

我为何对你钟情？

他们不知道我曾认识你，

曾经你了解很深：

我将长久哀叹你，

深沉得难以启口。

忆昔日幽会相见，

想今朝黯然悲伤，

你竟然把我淡忘，

你竟然把我欺骗，

倘若多年以后，

我们又邂逅相遇，

我该如何称呼你？

只有含着泪默默无语。

背景知识

乔治 · 戈登 · 拜伦 (George Gordon Byron)，英国浪漫主义文学的杰出代表。出生于伦敦破落的贵族家庭，10 岁继承男爵爵位。他曾在哈罗中学和剑桥大学读书，深受启蒙主义的熏陶。他是 19 世纪初欧洲革命运动中争取民主自由和民族解放的一名战士。也是英国诗坛上有争议的“怪人”和“浪子”。德国诗人哥德称之为“本世纪最伟大的才子诗人”。

这首诗回忆了与爱人分别时的情景和感受，以及后来的心情。“In silence and tears”的重复，前后呼应，真切感人；此外，较短的诗节和断开的句子，也暗示出难以压抑，无法平静的痛苦心境。

单词注解

thy [ðai]【古】你的 (thou 的所有格)

chill [tʃil] 寒冷，寒气

rue [ru:] 懊悔，后悔

名句诵读

When we two parted In silence and tears，Half broken-hearted To serve for years，Pale grew thy cheek and cold，Colder thy kiss，Truly that hour foretold Sorrow to this！

The dew of the morning Suck chill or my brow It felt like the warning Of what I feel now.

If I should meet thee After long years，How should I greet thee ? With silence and tears.

You Know My Heart

Bettine Brentano to Goethe

You know my heart;
You know that all there is desire,
Thought, **boding** and longing;
You live among spirits and they give you divine wisdom.
You must **nourish** me;
You give all that in advance,
Which I do not understand to ask for.

My mind has a small embrace,
My love a large one;
You must bring them to a balance.
Love cannot be quiet till the mind matches its growth;
You are matched to my love;
You are friendly, kind and **indulgent**;
Let me know when my heart is off the balance.
I understand your silent signs.

A look from your eyes into mine,
A kiss from you upon my lips,
Instructs me in all,

What might seem delighted to learn,
To one who, like me,
Had experience from those.
I am far from you;
Mine are become strange to me.

I must ever return in thought to that hour when you hold me in the soft fold of your arm.
Then I begin to weep,
But the tears dry again unawares.
Yes, he reaches with his love (thus I think) over to me in this concealed stillness;
And should not I, with my eternal undisturbed loving, reach to him in the distance?

Ah, conceive what my heart has to say to you;
It overflows with soft sighs all whisper to you.
Be my only happiness on earth your friendly will to me.
O, dear friend,
Give me but a sign that you are conscious of me.

你懂我的心

贝婷 · 布伦塔诺致歌德

你懂我的心；
你懂我心中所有的愿望
思念、预兆和渴求；
你生活在幽灵之中，
他们给你以神灵的智慧。
你一定要给我以“滋养”。
如你以前给予我的一样，
给予我无法诉求的向往。

虽说我才疏学浅，
但我的爱很博渊；
你一定要平衡这两方面。
在理智跟不上爱情的节奏时，便波浪连连。
你知道我有多爱你；
你友善、温存、宽厚。
告诉我，什么时候我的心失了衡。
我懂得你那无声的暗示。

你映入我眼帘的凝睇，
你印在我唇上的热吻，
向我说明了一切。
这一切对于像我这样的人，
对于有过这方面感情经历的人，
看来似乎令人高兴。
你我天各一方，
给你的凝望和亲吻，我已日益陌生。

我无法不想抱你入怀的温柔。
然后我便开始抽泣，
不知不觉眼泪已干涸。
是的，在深藏的静谧中他对我一往情深（我如是想）。
难道我就不应借着永不动摇的深情遥通心声吗?

啊，你不知道我一心要对你说的话?
我要对你无限地轻声叹息，窃窃私语，让感情满溢升华。
愿我今生今世唯一的幸福就是你对我的无限温柔。
啊，亲爱的朋友，
只求你给我暗示，你心中只有我一个人。

实战提升
Practising & Exercise

背景知识

约翰·沃尔夫冈·冯·歌德(Johann Wolfgang von Goethe)，18世纪中叶到19世纪初德国和欧洲最重要的剧作家、诗人、思想家，他一生跨两个世纪，正当欧洲社会大动荡大变革的年代。

这首诗是贝婷·布伦塔诺给歌德写的一封情书，被誉为“史上最经典的情书”。

单词注解

boding ['bəudiŋ] 预兆

nourish ['nʌriʃ] 养育；滋养

indulgent [in'dʌldʒənt] 宽容的；宽大的

overflow ['əuvə'fləu] 充满；洋溢

conscious ['kɔnʃəs] 意识到的，自觉的

名句诵读

My mind has a small embrace，My love a large one；You must bring them to a balance.

I am far from you；Mine are become strange to me.

O，dear friend，Give me but a sign that you are conscious of me.

The River-Merchant's Wife: A Letter

Li Bai

While my hair was still cut straight across my forehead
I played about the front gate, pulling flowers.
You came by on **bamboo** stilts, playing horse,
You walked about my seat, playing with blue plums.
And we went on living in the village of Chokan:
Two small people, without dislike or **suspicion**.
At fourteen I married My Lord you.
I never laughed, being bashful.
Lowering my head, I looked at the wall.
Called to, a thousand times, I never looked back.
At fifteen I stopped scowling,
I desired my dust to be mingled with yours
Forever and forever and forever.
Why should I climb the look out?
At sixteen you departed,
You went into far Ku-to-yen, by the river of swirling **eddies**,
And you have been gone five months.
The monkeys make sorrowful noise overhead.
You dragged your feet when you went out.
By the gate now, the moss is grown, the different mosses

Too deep to clear them away!

The leaves fall early this autumn, in wind.

The paired butterflies are already yellow with August,

Over the grass in the West garden;

They hurt me. I grow older.

If you are coming down through the narrows of the river Kiang,

Please let me know beforehand,

And I will come out to meet you

As far as Cho-fu-Sa.

长干行

李　白

妾发初覆额，折花门前剧。
郎骑竹马来，绕床弄青梅。
同居长干里，两小无嫌猜。
十四为君妇，羞颜未尝开。
低头向暗壁，千唤不一回。
十五始展眉，愿同尘与灰。
常存抱柱信，岂上望夫台。
十六君远行，瞿塘滟滪堆。
五月不可触，猿声天上哀。
门前旧行迹，一一生绿苔。
苔深不能扫，落叶秋风早。
八月蝴蝶黄，双飞西园草。
感此伤妾心，坐愁红颜老。
早晚下三巴，预将书报家。
相迎不道远，直至长风沙。

实战提升

Practising & Exercise

背景知识

李白（701–762），字太白，号青莲居士，又号“谪仙人”（贺知章评李白，李白亦自诩）。汉族，祖籍陇西成纪（现甘肃省静宁县），生于中亚西域的碎叶城（在今吉尔吉斯斯坦首都比什凯克以东的托克马克市附近），4岁迁居四川绵州昌隆县（今四川省江油市，这种说法以郭沫若为代表）。我国唐代伟大的浪漫主义诗人，被后人称为“诗仙”，与杜甫并称为“李杜”。其诗风格豪放飘逸洒脱，想象丰富，语言流转自然，音律和谐多变。

《长干行》属于乐府杂曲歌辞，原为长江下游一带的民歌。全诗使用第一人称的口吻，并运用年龄记叙和四季相思的民歌手法，巧妙地把女主人公的生活场景有机地串联在一起，形成了一个完整的艺术整体。通过这首诗，这位弱小的南国女子用“萦迂回折”的口吻，向我们坦露了她一生中平凡但却“一往情深”的感情经历。

单词注解

bamboo [bæm'bu:] 竹，竹子

suspicion [səs'piʃən] 怀疑，疑心

eddy ['edi] 旋涡；涡流

名句诵读

While my hair was still cut straight across my forehead I played about the front gate，pulling flowers.

At fifteen I stopped scowling，I desired my dust to be mingled with yours Forever and forever and forever.

The leaves fall early this autumn，in wind. The paired butterflies are already yellow with August，Over the grass in the West garden；They hurt me. I grow older.

When You Are Old

William Butler Yeats

When you are old and grey and full of sleep,
And **nodding** *by the fire, take down this book,*
And slowly read, and dream of the soft look
Your eyes had once, and of their **shadows** *deep;*

How many loved your moments of glad grace,
And loved your beauty with love false or true,
But one man loved the **pilgrim** soul in you,
And loved the sorrows of your changing face;

And bending down beside the glowing bars,
Murmur, a little sadly, how love fled
And paced upon the mountains overhead
And hid his face **amid** *a crowd of stars.*

当你老了

威廉 · 巴特勒 · 叶芝

当你老了，头发灰白，睡思昏沉，
炉火旁打盹，请取下这部诗歌，
慢慢读，回想你过去眼神中的柔和
回想它们过去的浓重的阴影；

多少人爱你优雅欢畅的时候
爱慕你的美貌，不论出于假意或真心，
只有一个人爱你那坚贞的灵魂，
爱你老去的容颜上那痛苦的皱纹。

躬身在红光闪耀的炉火旁，
凄然地低语，爱为何消逝，
在头顶的山上他缓缓踱着步子，
将脸隐没在了群星之中。

背景知识

威廉 · 巴特勒 · 叶芝 (William Butler Yeats)，爱尔兰诗人、剧作家，著名的神秘主义者。叶芝是“爱尔兰文艺复兴运动”的领袖。叶芝早年的诗作通常从爱尔兰神话和民间传说中取材，其语言风格则受到拉斐尔前派散文的影响，他曾被誉为“当代最伟大的诗人”。

1889 年 1 月 30 日，23 岁的叶芝遇见了美丽的女演员茅德 · 冈。诗人对她一见钟情，诗人对她的强烈爱慕之情给诗人带来了无穷的灵感，此后诗人创作了许多有关这方面的诗歌。《当你老了》就是其中一首。当时的叶芝还是一名穷学生，对爱情充满希望，对于感伤还只是一种假设和隐隐的感觉。因而这首诗没有跌宕起伏的激动和宣泄，只有朴素的语言、舒缓的调子、淡淡的感伤，娓娓道来的平静倾诉，让人感到异常亲切与温馨。据说水木年华的《一生有你》就是由这首诗的灵感而来：“多少人曾爱慕你年轻时的容颜，可知谁愿承受岁月无情的变迁，多少人曾在你生命中来了又还，可知一生有你我都陪在你身边。”

单词注解

nod [nɔd] 打盹，打瞌睡

shadow [ˈʃædəu] 影子，阴影

pilgrim [ˈpilgrim] 香客，朝圣者

amid [əˈmid] 在……之间；在……之中

名句诵读

When you are old and grey and full of sleep, And nodding by the fire, take down this book, And slowly read, and dream of the soft look Your eyes had once, and of their shadows deep;

And bending down beside the glowing bars, Murmur, a little sadly, how love fled And paced upon the mountains overhead And hid his face amid a crowd of stars.

Fortuitousness

Xu Zhimo

Being a cloud in the sky
On your heart lake I ***cast*** *my figure.*
You don't have to wonder.
Nor should you **cheer**
In an instant I will disappear.

On the dark sea we encounter
In different directions of our own we steer.
It's nice for you to remember.
But you'd better forget the ***luster***
That we've been devoted to cach other.

偶　然

徐志摩

我是天空里的一片云，
偶尔投影在你的波心
你不必讶异；
更无须欢喜
在转瞬间消灭了踪影。

你我相逢在黑夜的海上，
你有你的，我有我的，方向；
你记得也好，
最好你忘掉，
在这交会时互放的光芒。

实战提升
Practising & Exercise

背景知识

徐志摩（1897 ~ 1931），现代诗人、散文家。他的诗字句清新，韵律谐和，比喻新奇，想象丰富，意境优美，神思飘逸，富于变化，并追求艺术形式的整饬、华美，具有鲜明的艺术个性，为新月派的代表诗人。他的散文也自成一格，取得了不亚于诗歌的成就，其中不少都是传世的名篇。

作者在这首诗中把“偶然”这样一个极为抽象的时间副词，使之形象化，置入象征性的结构，充满情趣哲理，不但珠圆玉润，朗朗上口，而且余味无穷，意溢于言外。这首诗在徐志摩诗美追求的历程中，还具有一些独特的“转折”性意义。这首诗后来由香港歌手陈秋霞作曲并演唱。

单词注解

cast [kɑ:st] 投，抛

cheer [tʃiə] 愉快，欢呼

luster [ˈlʌstə] 光彩，光泽

名句诵读

Being a cloud in the sky On your heart lake I cast my figure. You don' t have to wonder.

On the dark sea we encounter In different directions of our own we steer. It's nice for you to remember. But you'd better forget the luster That we've been devoted to cach other.

The Love Song of J. Alfred Prufrock

T.S.Eliot

Let us go then, you and I,
When the evening is spread out against the sky
Like a patient **etherized** upon a table;
Let us go, through certain half-deserted streets,
The muttering **retreats**
Of restless nights in one-night cheap hotels
And sawdust restaurants with oyster shells:
Streets that follow like a **tedious** argument
Of insidious intent
To lead you to an overwhelming question ...
Oh, do not ask, "What is it?"
Let us go and make our visit.

In the room the women come and go
Talking of Michelangelo.

The yellow fog that rubs its back upon the window panes,
The yellow smoke that rubs its **muzzle** on the window panes
Licked its tongue into the corners of the evening,
Lingered upon the pools that stand in drains,

Let fall upon its back the soot that falls from chimneys,
Slipped by the terrace, made a sudden leap,
And seeing that it was a soft October night,
Curled once about the house, and fell asleep.

And indeed there will be time
For the yellow smoke that slides along the street,
Rubbing its back upon the window panes;
There will be time, there will be time
To prepare a face to meet the faces that you meet;
There will be time to murder and create,
And time for all the works and days of hands
That lift and drop a question on your plate;
Time for you and time for me,
And time yet for a hundred indecisions,
And for a hundred visions and revisions,
Before the taking of a toast and tea.

In the room the women come and go
Talking of Michelangelo.

And indeed there will be time
To wonder, "Do I dare?" and, "Do I dare?"
Time to turn back and descend the stair,
With a bald spot in the middle of my hair—
[They will say, "How his hair is growing thin!"]
My morning coat, my collar mounting firmly to the chin,
My necktie rich and modest, but asserted by a simple pin—
[They will say, "But how his arms and legs are thin!"]

Do I dare
Disturb the universe?
In a minute there is time
For decisions and revisions which a minute will reverse.

For I have known them all already, known them all—
Have known the evenings, mornings, afternoons,
I have measured out my life with coffee spoons;
I know the voices dying with a dying fall
Beneath the music from a farther room.
So how should I presume?

And I have known the eyes already, known them all—
The eyes that fix you in a formulated phrase,
And when I am formulated, sprawling on a pin,
When I am pinned and wriggling on the wall,
Then how should I begin
To spit out all the butt-ends of my days and ways?
And how should I presume?

And I have known the arms already, known them all—
Arms that are braceleted and white and bare
[But in the lamplight, downed with light brown hair!]
Is it perfume from a dress
That makes me so digress?
Arms that lie along a table, or wrap about a shawl.
And should I then presume?
And how should I begin?

...

Shall I say, I have gone at dusk through narrow streets
And watched the smoke that rises from the pipes
Of lonely men in shirt-sleeves, leaning out of windows? ...

I should have been a pair of ragged **claws**
Scuttling across the floors of silent seas.

...

And the afternoon, the evening, sleeps so peacefully!
Smoothed by long fingers,
Asleep ... tired ... or it malingers,
Stretched on the floor, here beside you and me.
Should I, after tea and cakes and ices
Have the strength to force the moment to its crisis?

But though I have wept and fasted, wept and prayed,
Though I have seen my head [grown slightly bald] brought in
upon a platter
I am no prophet—and here's no great matter;
I have seen the moment of my greatness flicker,
And I have seen the eternal Footman hold my coat, and snicker,
And in short, I was afraid.

And would it have been worth it, after all,
After the cups, the marmalade, the tea,
Among the porcelain, among some talk of you and me,
Would it have been worth while,
To have bitten off the matter with a smile,
To have squeezed the universe into a ball
To roll it toward some overwhelming question,

To say, "I am Lazarus, come from the dead
Come back to tell you all, I shall tell you all" —
If one, settling a pillow by her head,
Should say: "That is not what I meant at all.
That is not it, at all."

And would it have been worth it, after all,
Would it have been worth while,
After the sunsets and the dooryards and the sprinkled streets,
After the novels, after the teacups, after the skirts that trail
along the
floor–
And this, and so much more? —
It is impossible to say just what I mean!
But as if a magic lantern threw the nerves in patterns on a
screen:
Would it have been worth while
If one, settling a pillow or throwing off a shawl,
And turning toward the window, should say:
"That is not it at all,
That is not what I meant, at all."
…
No! I am not Prince Hamlet, or was meant to be;
Am an attendant lord one that will do
To swell a progress, start a scene or two,
Advise the prince; no doubt, an easy tool,
Deferential, glad to be of use,
Politic, cautious, and meticulous;
Full of high sentence, but a bit obtuse

At times，indeed，almost ridiculous —
Almost，at times，the Fool.

I grow old... I grow old...
I shall wear the bottoms of my trousers rolled.

Shall I part my hair behind? Do I dare to eat a peach?
I shall wear white flannel trousers，and walk upon the beach.
I have heard the mermaids singing，each to each.
I do not think that they will sing to me.

I have seen them riding seaward on the waves
Combing the white hair of the waves blown back
When the wind blows the water white and black.

We have lingered in the chambers of the sea
By sea-girls wreathed with seaweed red and brown
Till human voices wake us，and we drown.

阿尔弗瑞德 · 普鲁弗洛克的情歌

T·S·艾略特

那么我们走吧，我们一起，
此时黄昏正在延展，佣向天际
像麻醉的病人躺在手术台上；
我们走吧，穿过一些半冷清的街，
那儿休憩的场所正人声喋喋；
有夜夜不宁的便宜歇夜旅店
露天的餐馆里牡蛎壳遍地，
街连着街，好像一场冗长的争议
怀着阴险的目的
要把你引向一个重大的问题……
噢，别问“是什么？”
让我们去走访一遍。

客厅里女人来来回回穿梭，
正在谈论着米开朗琪罗

黄色的雾在窗玻璃上擦着它的背，
黄色的烟在窗玻璃上擦着它的嘴，

它的舌头伸进黄昏的角落，舔过以后
就在干涸的水池上面徘徊。
让烟囱里的烟灰落在它的脊背，
滑过斜坡地，蓦然一跃，
发现正值温柔的十月夜晚，
于是在房屋附近蜷伏起来，安然睡觉。

呵，确实地，总会有时间
看黄色的烟沿着街滑行，
在窗玻璃上擦着它的背；
总会有时间，总会有时间
准备一副面容去会见你见的那个人；
总会有时间去谋杀，去创新，
有时间去做天天的手头活计；
在你的茶盘上提起或放下一个问题；
有的是时间，无论你，无论我，
还有的是时间犹疑一百遍，
有时间幻想一百遍，修正一百遍，
然后再去吃茶点。

客厅里女人来来回回穿梭，
正在谈论着米开朗琪罗

呵，确实地，总还有时间
来疑问，“我可有勇气？”“我可有勇气？”
总还有时间来转身走下楼梯，

把一块秃顶暴露给人去注意——
（她们会说："他的头发长得真稀！）
我的晨礼服，挺立到下巴的衣领，
我的领带雅致而多彩，用简朴别针固定——
（她们会说："但他的手臂和腿瘦骨伶仃！"）
我可有勇气
搅乱这个宇宙？
在一分钟里总还有时间
决定和变卦，过一分钟还可推翻。

因为我已经熟悉了她们，并且了如指掌——
熟悉了那些黄昏，和上下午的情景，
我是用咖啡匙子量出了我的生命；
我知道每当隔壁响起了音乐
话声就逐渐低微而至停歇。
所以我怎么敢提出？

而且我已熟悉那些眼睛，熟悉了一切——
那些用一句公式化的成语把你钉住的眼睛，
当我被公式化了，在钉针下趴伏，
当我被钉着在墙壁上挣扎，
那么我将如何开始
吐出我一生岁月习惯中所有的残渣？
因此我该怎样冒昧提起？

而且我已经熟悉那些胳膊，熟悉了一切——

那些胳膊戴着镯子，又袒露又白净
（可是在灯光下，显得淡褐色毛茸茸！）
是否由于衣裙的香气
使得我这样话离本题?
那些手臂横放在桌上，或用披巾卷起。
那时候我该提出吗?
可是我怎么开口?
……
我是否说，黄昏时穿过几条小街，
看到孤独的男子只穿着衬衫
倚在窗口，烟斗里冒着袅袅的烟? ……

我倒不如做一对粗俗的蟹爪
匆匆爬过静寂的海底。
……

啊，那下午，那黄昏，睡得多平静！
被纤长的手指轻轻抚爱，
睡了……疲倦了……或者佯装有病，
躺在地板上，就在你我脚边伸开。
是否我，在用过茶、糕点和冷饮以后，
我是否有勇气把这一刻推向紧要关头?

然而，尽管我曾哭泣斋戒，哭泣祈祷，
尽管我看见我的头（有点秃顶）用盘子端过来，
我不是先知——这也不值得大惊小怪；

我曾看到我伟大的时刻在动摇，
我曾看到那永恒的“侍者”拿着我的外衣暗笑，
简而言之，我感到害怕。

而且，归根到底，那是否值得，
在用过茶点，吃过果酱以后，
在杯盘中间，当人们谈着你和我，
是不是值得以一个微笑
把这件事情一口啃掉，
把整个宇宙压缩成一个球，
使它滚向一个重大的问题，
说道：“我是拉撒路，从死人那里
来报一个信，我要告诉你们一切”——
万一她拿个枕头垫在脑下，
竟然说：“那根本不是我的意思。
不是的，那根本不是。”

那么，归根到底，是不是值得，
是否值得在那许多次夕阳以后，
在庭院的散步和水淋过街道以后，
在读小说以后，在饮茶以后，在长裙拖过地板以后——
说这些，和许多许多事情？——
但不可能真正说出我的意图！
仿佛有盏神灯把神经活动图投射到屏幕上：
是否值得，假如
她在头下垫个枕头，脱去披风，

把头转向窗户，说道：
“不是的，根本不是，
那根本不是我的意思。”
……

不！我不是哈姆雷特王子，也无此意；
我只是个侍从爵士，能逢场作戏，
能为一两个景开场，或为王子出主意，
就够好的了；无非是顺手的工具，
恭恭敬敬，乐于听人使唤，
彬彬有礼，小心翼翼，仔仔细细；
满口高调，但有点愚钝不灵利；
有时，几乎实在滑稽可笑——
有时，近乎一个丑角。

呵，我变老了……我变老了……
我将要把我的裤脚边卷起。

我是否把头发从后面分开？我可敢吃桃？
我将要穿上白色法兰绒裤，去海滨漫步。
美人鱼在对歌，她们的歌声我已听到。
但我想她们不是唱给我听。

我已经看到她们乘着波浪游向海里，
梳理着被冲回的浪涛白头，
当海风把海水刮得黑白交加。

我们在海宫中流连忘返，
水仙子用红褐水草把大海装饰如此美丽，
一旦被人声唤醒，我们就淹死。

背景知识

T·S· 艾略特（T.S.Eliot），英国著名现代派诗人和文艺评论家。1888 年 9 月 26 日生于美国密苏里州。1906 年入哈佛大学学哲学，续到英国上牛津大学，后留英教书和当职员。1908 年开始创作。代表作《荒原》，表达了西方一代人精神上的幻灭，被认为是西方现代文学中具有划时代意义的作品。1948 年因“革新现代诗，功绩卓著的先驱”，获诺贝尔文学奖。

诗人通过诗中的主人公普鲁弗洛克的无望的虚幻的求爱过程，描述了一种普遍存在的病态世象，从而唱响了精神瘫痪、文明衰退，到处充满意志消沉、无所事事的“活死人”的黄昏世界的哀歌。

单词注解

etherize ['i:θəraiz] 麻醉
retreat [ri'tri:t] 僻静，安静
tedious ['ti:diəs] 冗长乏味的；使人厌烦的
muzzle ['mʌzl] 动物的口鼻部
claw [klɔ:] 爪，脚爪

名句诵读

And the afternoon, the evening, sleeps so peacefully! Smoothed by long fingers, Asleep ... tired ... or it malingers, Stretched on the floor, here beside you and me.

I grow old... I grow old... I shall wear the bottoms of my trousers rolled.

We have lingered in the chambers of the sea By sea-girls wreathed with seaweed red and brown Till human voices wake us, and we drown.

I Loved You

Alexander Sergeyevich Pushkin

I loved you;

*even now I may **confess,***

*Some embers of my love their fire **retain**;*

But do not let it cause you more distress,

I do not want to sadden you again.

Hopeless and tongue-tied, yet I loved you dearly

*With pangs the jealous and the **timid** know;*

So tenderly I loved you, so sincerely,

I pray God grant another love you so.

我曾经爱过你

亚历山大·谢尔盖耶维奇·普希金

我曾经爱过你：爱情，也许
在我的心灵里还没有完全消亡，
但愿它不会再打扰你，
我也不想再使你难过悲伤。

我曾经默默无语、毫无指望地爱过你，
我既忍受着羞怯，又忍受着嫉妒的折磨，
我曾经那样真诚、那样温柔地爱过你，
但愿上帝保佑你，
另一个人也会像我爱你一样。

背景知识

亚历山大·谢尔盖耶维奇·普希金（Alexander Sergeyevich Pushkin），俄国著名的文学家、伟大的诗人、小说家及现代俄国文学的创始人，19世纪俄国浪漫主义文学的主要代表，同时也是现实主义文学的奠基人，现代标准俄语的创始人，被誉为“俄国文学之父”、“俄国诗歌的太阳”。他的作品是俄国民族意识高涨以及贵族革命运动在文学上的反映。

这首诗是献给安娜·阿列克谢耶夫娜·奥列尼娜的。奥列尼娜是美术学院院长、彼得堡公共图书馆馆长、考古学家奥列宁的千金小姐。1828年夏天，普希金很想和奥列尼娜结为夫妻，但却遭到了她的父亲的拒绝。普希金遭到拒绝后，很快离开了彼得堡。后来，普希金疏远了与奥列尼娜一家的关系，其中很重要的原因是她的父亲越来越靠近沙皇，而且对社会上流传的普希金的讽刺短诗极为不满。

单词注解

confess [kən'fes] 坦白，供认
retain [ri'tein] 保留，保持
timid ['timid] 胆小的，羞怯的

名句诵读

I loved you；even now I may confess，Some embers of my love their fire retain；But do not let it cause you more distress，I do not want to sadden you again.

Hopeless and tongue-tied，yet I loved you dearly With pangs the jealous and the timid know；So tenderly I loved you，so sincerely，I pray God grant another love you so.

If You Forget Me

Pablo Neruda

I want you to know one thing
You know how this is
If I look at the crystal moon
at the red branch
of the slow autumn at my window.
If I touch near the fire
the **impalpable** ash,
or the wrinkled body of the log
Everything carries me to you
As if everything that exists
Aromas, light, medals,
Or little boats that sail toward
those isles of your that wait for me,
Well now. If little by little
You stop loving me,
I shall stop loving you
Little by little.
If suddenly you forget me
Do not look for me
For I shall already have forgotten you.

If you think it long and mad
the wind of banners
that passes through my life,
And you decide to leave me
at the shore of the heart where I have roots,
Remember, that on that day, at that hour,
I shall lift my arms
And my roots will set off
to seek another land.
But, if each day, each hour,
You feel that you are **destined** for me
with **implacable** aweerness,
If each day a flower climbs
up to your lips to seek me,
Ah my love, ah my own,
in me all that fire is repeated,
In me nothing is **extinguished** or forgotten
My love feeds on your love, beloved,
And as long as you live
it will be in your arms without leaving mine.

如果你忘了我

帕布罗 · 聂鲁达

希望你知道
这是我的想法
当我凭窗凝望
姗姗而来的秋日
红枝上的明月
当我轻触火堆旁
似有似无的尘烬
或是褶皱层层的木柴
我的心儿就会飞向你
似乎一切都有了
芬芳、光明和荣誉
就像小舟荡向岛屿
那里，你等候着我
然而，假若
你对我的爱情淡去
我的爱火也会
渐渐熄灭。
如果瞬间你忘了我

别来找我，
因为我早已把你忘怀。
我生命中
过往的猎猎疾风
如果你嫌它过于悠长，过于疯狂
而决意离我而去。
在我爱情所深埋的心之岸
记住，彼时彼刻，
我将举起双臂
摇断爱的根脉，
憩于地方。
但是，如果每时每刻
如果你也感觉到你是我的真命天子
能共享奇妙的甜蜜
如果你迎向我的红唇
每天绽若鲜花
啊，我的爱人，我心里
所有的爱火将再度燃起，
永不会消失，永不被忘记
我的情因你的爱而生，爱人啊
情长今生，
不离你我臂弯。

背景知识

帕布罗 · 聂鲁达（Pablo Neruda），智利著名诗人，1971 年诺贝尔文学奖得主。他在少年时代就喜爱写诗并起笔名为聂鲁达，16 岁入圣地亚哥智利教育学院学习法语。1928 年进入外交界任驻外领事、大使等职。1945 年被选为国会议员，并获智利国家文学奖，同年加入智利共产党。他曾当选为世界和平理事会理事，获斯大林国际和平奖金。

诗人在这首诗里展现了爱情中表现出来的“等待”的维度。在该诗“等待”的爱情观中的“我”是外向型的，表现为大胆、狂热的追求倾向，带着野性的向心力去表达自我的情感，即使对方是虚幻的、无望的，还是照样展示出自己的豁达与开朗。

单词注解

impalpable [im'pælpəbl] 无法感触到的；无形的
destined ['destind] 命中注定的
implacable [im'plækəbl] 难平息的；难和解的；
extinguish [iks'tiŋgwiʃ] 灭绝，熄灭

名句诵读

If I look at the crystal moon at the red branch of the slow autumn at my window.

Do not look for me For I shall already have forgotten you.

My love feeds on your love，beloved，And as long as you live it will be in your arms without leaving mine.

Song to Celia

Ben Jonson

Drink to me only with thine eyes,
And I will **pledge** *with mine;*
Or leave a kiss but in the cup,
And I'll not look for wine.
The thirst that from the soul doth rise
Doth ask a drink divine;
But might I of Jove's nectar sup,
I would not change for thine.

I sent thee late a rosy wreath,
Not so much honouring thee
As giving it a hope, that there
It could not wither'd be.
But thou **thereon didst** *only breathe,*
And sent'st it back to me;
Since when it grows, and smells, I swear,
Not of itself, but thee.

致西丽娅

本 · 琼森

你只用你的双眸与我干杯
我回以脉脉的温存
或在杯边留下你的香吻
我心将不再向往杯中蜜酿
心灵的渴望在荡漾
渴望你的仙酿
即使天神让我将他的琼浆痛饮，
我也不愿舍弃你吻过的这杯。

曾忆赠你玫瑰花环
并非讨你欢心
只愿这花环在你头上
永不凋零。
只要你的气息留在上面
然后将玫瑰送还
当盛开时，它让我闻到的，
不是自己的花香，而是你。

背景知识

本 · 琼森（Ben Jonson），英国文艺复兴时期重要的剧作家、诗人和评论家。1572年6月11日生于伦敦。主要诗集有《格言诗》、《森林集》、《灌木集》等。他曾就学于古代史学者坎姆登，并在其资助下到威斯敏斯特学校读书，获得关于希腊、罗马文学的丰富知识。后来，他博览群书，成为当时学识最渊博的剧作家之一。

这首诗中，热恋中的情郎手端美酒，眼睛却在寻找与情人沟通的机会。玫瑰花冠是爱情的象征，但情郎此举不只是为了取悦情人或纯粹地表达爱意，而是为了让玫瑰花接受情人的亲吻后得以“永不凋残”，并且就如同情人的气息般永远地保留在自己的记忆中！真可谓情之深，爱之切。诗人对情郎的心理描写得细致入微，字里行间流露出真挚情意。

单词注解

pledge [pledʒ] 保证，誓言
thereon [ðεə'ɔn] 在其上
didst [didst]【古诗】=did

名句诵读

Drink to me only with thine eyes，And I will pledge with mine；Or leave a kiss but in the cup，And I'll not look for wine.

I sent thee late a rosy wreath，Not so much honouring thee As giving it a hope，that there It could not wither'd be.

Since when it grows，and smells，I swear，Not of itself，but thee.

A Blooming Tree

Xi Murong

May **Buddha** let us meet
in my most beautiful hours,

I have prayed for it
for five hundred years.
Buddha made me a tree
by the path you may take,

In full blossoms I'm waiting in the sun
every flower carrying my ***previous*** *hope.*

As you are near, listen carefully
the quivering leaves are my waiting **zeal**,

As you pass by the tree
without noticing me,
My friend, upon the ground behind you
is not the fallen ***petals*** *but my withered heart.*

一棵开花的树

席慕容

如何让你遇见我
在我最美丽的时刻

为这
我已在佛前求了五百年
求佛让我们结一段尘缘
佛于是把我化做一棵树
长在你必经的路旁

阳光下
慎重地开满了花
朵朵都是我前世的盼望

当你走近
请你细听
那颤抖的叶
是我等待的热情

而当你终于无视地走过

在你身后落了一地的

朋友啊

那不是花瓣

那是我凋零的心

背景知识

席慕蓉(1943.10.15—　)女，蒙古族，著名诗人、散文家、画家。席慕蓉全名是穆伦・席连勃，意即大江河，“慕蓉”是“穆伦”的谐译。她写诗，为的是“纪念一段远去的岁月，纪念那个只曾在我心中存在过的小小世界”。一个“真”字熔铸于诗中而又个性鲜明。在她的诗中，充满着一种对人情、爱情、乡情的悟性和理解。著作有诗集、散文集、画册及选本等五十余种，读者遍及海内外。近十年来，潜心探索蒙古文化，以原乡为创作主题。

这首诗成功地突出了抒情主人公与开花的树、物与我的关系，凝聚成传情达意的意象群落，以及将感受视听化的艺术效果，读之不由人不叹息。尤其是，一棵树，“阳光下慎重地开满了花”，极具画面感，极具视觉冲击力，几乎开在读者心里，让人过目难忘。全诗体现的总体风格是宁静、执着。在看似平淡的语气下，是波澜起伏的心的大海。这心海的波澜将一直为着爱而潮起潮落——尽管这爱也许是绝望的。

单词注解

Buddha ['budə] 佛；佛像
previous ['pri:vjəs] 先的，前的
zeal [zi:l] 热心；热诚
petal ['petl] 花瓣

名句诵读

I have prayed for it for five hundred years.

In full blossoms I'm waiting in the sun every flower carrying my previous hope.

As you pass by the tree without noticing me, My friend, upon the ground behind you is not the fallen petals but my withered heart.

Love at First Sight

Wislawa Szymborska

They're both ***convinced***
that a sudden passion joined them.
Such certainty is beautiful,
but uncertainty is more beautiful still

Since they'd never met before, they're sure
that there'd been nothing between them.
But what's the word from the streets, staircases, hallways...
perhaps they've passed each other a million times?

I want to ask them
if they don't remember...
a moment face to face
in some revolving door?
perhaps a "sorry" muttered in a crowd?
a curt "wrong number" caught in the receiver?
but I know the answer.
No, they don't remember .

They'd be **amazed** to hear
that Chance has been toying with them

now for years.
Not quite ready yet
to become their Destiny,
it pushed them close, drove them apart,
it barred their path,
stifling a laugh,
and then leaped aside.

There were signs and signals,
even if they couldn't read them yet.
Perhaps three years ago
or just last Tuesday
a certain leaf **fluttered**
from one shoulder to another?

Something was dropped and then picked up.
Who knows, maybe the ball that vanished
into childhood's thicket?
There were doorknobs and doorbells
where one touch had covered another
beforehand.

Suitcases checked and standing side by side.
One night, perhaps, the same dream,
grown **hazy** by morning.

Every beginning
is only a sequel, after all,
and the book of events
is always open halfway through.

一见钟情

维斯拉瓦 · 辛波丝卡

他们彼此深信
是瞬间迸发的热情使他们相遇
这样的笃定是美丽的
但变幻无常更为美丽

他们素未谋面，所以他们确定彼此并无瓜葛。
但是自街道、楼梯、大堂传来的话语……
他们也许擦肩而过一百万次了吧。

我想问他们
是否记得……
在旋转门
面对面那一刹
或是在人群中喃喃道出的“对不起”，
或是在电话的另一端道出的“打错了”。
但是我早知道答案。
是的，他们并不记得。

他们会很惊讶，
徜若得知缘分已经玩弄他们多年。
只因为尚未完全准备好，
他们的命运之神未来到，
缘分将他们拉近，驱离。
阻挡着他们的去路
憋住笑声
然后闪到一旁。

有一些迹象和信号存在，
即使他们尚无法解读。
也许在三年前
或者就在上个星期二，
有某片叶子飘舞于
肩与肩之间?

有东西掉了又捡了起来?
天晓得，也许是那个
消失于童年灌木丛中的球?
还有事前已被触摸
层层覆盖的
门把和门铃。

检查完毕后并排放置的手提箱。
有一晚，也许同样的梦，
到了早晨变得模糊。

每个开始

毕竟都只是续篇，

而充满情节的书本

总是从一半开始看起。

背景知识

维斯拉瓦・辛波丝卡 (Wislawa Szymborska)，波兰女诗人。1996 年诺贝尔文学奖得主。她是第三位获得诺贝尔文学奖的女诗人、第四位获得诺贝尔文学奖的波兰作家，也是当今波兰最受欢迎的女诗人。她的诗作具有高度的严谨性及严肃性，在波兰拥有广大的读者群。

在这首诗里，我们看到人与人之间的微妙关系：两个素昧平生的人偶然相识，擦出火花，然而这真的是第一次相见吗？诗人使我们用全新的角度去看待疏离的人际关系，并且感受到一丝暖意和甜蜜。喜欢几米绘本《向左走，向右走》的朋友，一定不会忘记这首诗吧？

单词注解

convinced [kən'vinst] 确信的
amazed [ə'meizd] 吃惊的
flutter ['flʌtə] 飘动，飘扬
hazy ['heizi] 模糊的，朦胧的

名句诵读

They're both convinced that a sudden passion joined them. Such certainty is beautiful，but uncertainty is more beautiful still

There were signs and signals，even if they couldn't read them yet.

Every beginning is only a sequel，after all，and the book of events is always open halfway through.

………… Sadness of August …………

八月的忧愁

The Pride of Youth

Walter Scott

Proud Maisie is in the wood,
Walking so early;
Sweet Robin sits on the **bush***,*
Singing so rarely.

"Tell me，thou bonny bird，
when shall I marry me?"
— "When six braw gentlemen
Kirkward shall carry ye."

"Who makes the **bridal** *bed,*
Birdie，say truly?"
— "The gray-headed **sexton**
That delves the grave duly.

"The glowworm o'er grave and stone
Shall light thee steady;
The owl from the **steeple** *sing,*
Welcome，proud lady."

青春的骄傲

瓦尔特·司各特

骄傲的梅西漫步林间，
踩着晨曦；
伶俐的知更鸟栖息树丛，
唱得甜蜜。

“告诉我，美丽的鸟儿，
我哪年哪月穿嫁衣？”——
“等到六个殡葬人
抬你上教堂。”

“谁为我铺新床？
好鸟儿，莫撒谎。”——
“白发司事，兼挖墓穴，
误不了你的洞房。”

“萤火虫幽幽闪闪，
把你的坟墓照亮，
猫头鹰将在塔尖高唱：
欢迎你，骄傲的姑娘。”

背景知识

瓦尔特 · 司各特（Walter Scott），英国著名的历史小说家和诗人。他十分欣赏德国的“狂飙文学”，翻译过德国著名民谣《莱诺尔》。司各特的诗充满浪漫的冒险故事，深受读者欢迎。但当时拜伦的诗才遮蔽了司各特的才华，司各特转向小说创作，从而首创英国历史小说，为英国文学提供了 30 多部历史小说巨著。司各特的创作对欧洲历史小说起了开创作用，被尊为历史小说的创始人。英国的狄更斯、斯蒂文森，法国的雨果、巴尔扎克、大仲马，俄国的普希金，意大利的曼佐尼，美国的库柏等著名作家都曾受到司各特的深刻影响。

单词注解

bush [buʃ] 灌木，灌木丛
bridal ['braidl] 新娘的；婚礼的
sexton ['sekstən] 教堂司事
steeple ['sti:pl] 尖塔；尖顶

名句诵读

Proud Maisie is in the wood，Walking so early；Sweet Robin sits on the bush，Singing so rarely.

“Who makes the bridal bed，Birdie，say truly?” — “The gray-headed sexton That delves the grave duly.

“The glowworm o’er grave and stone Shall light thee steady；The owl from the steeple sing，Welcome，proud lady.”

Elegy Written in a Country Churchyard

Thomas Gray

The curfew tolls the knell of parting day,
The lowing herd wind slowly o' er the ***lea****.*
The plowman homeward plods his weary way,
And leaves the world to darkness and to me.

Now fades the glimmering landscape on the sight,
And all the air a solemn stillness holds,
Save where the beetle wheels his droning flight,
And drowsy tinklings lull the distant folds;

Save that from yonder ivy-mantled tower
The moping owl does to the moon complain
Of such, as wandering near her secret bower,
Molest her ancient solitary reign.

Beneath those rugged elms, that yew tree's shade,
Where heaves the turf in many a mouldering heap,
Each in his narrow cell forever laid,
The rude forefathers of the hamlet sleep.

The breezy call of incense-breathing morn,
The swallow twittering from the straw-built shed,
The cock's shrill clarion, or the echoing horn,
No more shall rouse them from their lowly bed.

For them no more the blazing hearth shall burn,
Or busy housewife ply her evening care;
No children run to lisp their sire's return,
Or climb his knees the envied kiss to share.

Oft did the harvest to their sickle yield,
Their furrow oft the stubborn **glebe** has broke;
How jocund did they drive their team afield!
How bowed the woods beneath their **sturdy** stroke!

Let not Ambition mock their useful toil,
Their homely joys, and destiny obscure;
Nor Grandeur hear with a **disdainful** smile,
The short and simple **annals** of the poor.

The boast of heraldry, the pomp of power,
And all that beauty, all that wealth e'er gave,
Awaits alike the inevitable hour.
The paths of glory lead but to the grave.

写在教堂墓地的挽歌

托马斯 · 格雷

黄昏时分敲响了晚钟，
牛羊在草地上鸣叫归笼。
农夫疲惫地走在回家的路上，
把整个世界留给了黄昏与我。

大地微光正慢慢消尽，
四周肃穆宁静。
只有甲壳虫在空中飞舞，
昏沉的铃声催眠着远处的羊栏。

还有那长满青藤的塔楼上，
一只忧郁的猫头鹰对月亮发着怨气。
说有人走近了她秘密的闺房，
扰乱了她那悠久而幽静的领地。

峥嵘的榆树底下，紫杉的绿荫里，
累累荒冢在绿草中隆起。
个个都长眠在小小的幽室中，

小村里粗鄙的父老在那里安睡。

芬芳的晨风在轻唤，
茅屋的燕语在呢喃。
号角回荡，雄鸡高啼，
再也不能把他们唤出九泉。

熊熊的灶火不再为他们而燃烧，
主妇也不再为他们做晚饭。
孩子们也不再迎接父亲的到来，
也不会再趴到父亲的膝上索吻撒娇。

过去他们常拿镰刀去收割庄稼，
顽梗的泥板让他们犁出了垄沟；
一棵棵树木在他们刀下放倒，
赶着牲口下地，他们是何等的欣喜！

有抱负的人别嘲笑他们的辛苦，
他们的欢乐太家常，他们的命运太寻常。
高贵的人也勿对他们冷笑，
来听听穷人们简约的“家国兴亡”。

无论什么炫耀的功勋与权势，
无论美丑，无论贫富，
大限之时准不一样。
极度荣光也是通往坟墓。

背景知识

托马斯 · 格雷 (Thomas Gray)，英国新古典主义后期的重要诗人，“墓畔派”的代表人物。他出生在伦敦的一个经纪人家庭，一生中的大部分时间在剑桥大学从事教学与研究工作。他的生活可谓中规中矩，捷足而又稳健。

这首诗通过对乡村一处墓地的描写，表达对那些默默无闻的人民的深切同情。作者赞扬了他们淳朴善良的品质，为他们没有机会施展天赋和才华而惋惜，同时也表现了对权贵、人间虚荣的蔑视和嘲讽，对大人物傲慢奢侈生活的谴责。

单词注解

lea [li:] 草原，牧草地
glebe [gli:b] 土地；旱田
sturdy ['stə:di] 健壮的，结实的；
disdainful [dis'deinful] 轻蔑的；骄傲的
annal ['ænl] 记录

名句诵读

The curfew tolls the knell of parting day，The lowing herd wind slowly o'er the lea.

The breezy call of incense-breathing morn，The swallow twittering from the straw-built shed，The cock's shrill clarion，or the echoing horn，No more shall rouse them from their lowly bed.

The boast of heraldry，the pomp of power，And all that beauty，all that wealth e'er gave，Awaits alike the inevitable hour. The paths of glory lead but to the grave.

Ode on a Grecian Urn

John Keats

Thou still unravished bride of quietness,
Thou foster-child of silence and slow time,
Sylvan historian, who canst thus express
A flowery tale more sweetly than our rhyme:
What leaf-fringed legend haunts about thy shape
Of deities or mortals, or of both,
In Tempe or the dales of Arcady?
What men or gods are these? What maidens loath?
What mad pursuit? What struggle to escape?
What pipes and **timbrels**? What wild ecstasy?

Heard melodies are sweet, but those unheard
Are sweeter; therefore, ye soft pipes, play on;
Not to the sensual ear, but, more endeared,
Pipe to the spirit dities of no tone:
Fair youth, beneath the trees, thou canst not leave
Thy song, nor ever can those trees be bare;
Bold Lover, never, never canst thou kiss,
Though winning near the goal—yet, do not grieve;
She cannot fade, though thou hast not thy bliss,

Forever wilt thou love, and she be fair!

Ah, happy, happy boughs! that cannot shed
Your leaves, nor ever bid the Spring **adieu**;
And, happy melodist, unwearied,
Forever piping songs forever new;
More happy love! more happy, happy love!
Forever warm and still to be enjoyed,
Forever panting, and forever young;
All breathing human passion far above,
That leaves a heart high-sorrowful and cloyed,
A burning forehead, and a parching tongue.

Who are these coming to the sacrifice?
To what green altar, O mysterious priest,
Lead'st thou that **heifer** lowing at the skies,
And all her silken flanks with garlands dressed?
What little town by river or sea-shore,
Or mountain-built with peaceful citadel,
Is emptied of this folk, this pious morn?
And, little town, thy streets for evermore
Will silent be; and not a soul to tell
Why thou art desolate, can e'er return.

O Attic shape! Fair attitude! with brede
Of marble men and **maidens** overwrought,
With forest branches and the trodden weed;
Thou, silent form, dost tease us out of thought
As doth eternity. Cold Pastoral!

When old age shall this generation waste,
Thou shalt remain, in midst of other woe
Than ours, a friend to man, to whom thou say'st,
"Beauty is truth, truth beauty," —that is all
Ye know on earth, and all ye need to know.

希腊古瓮颂

约翰·济慈

你仍是宁静未过门的新娘，
你是寂静与悠长岁月的养女，
呵，田园的史家，你竟能如此描述
一个如花的故事，比诗还瑰丽：
在你的形体上，岂非缭绕着
古老的传说，以绿叶为其边缘；
讲着人或神，敦陂或阿卡狄？
呵，是什么人，什么神！在舞乐前
多热烈地追求！少女怎样地逃！
又是怎样的笛子和手鼓？怎样狂野地着迷？

乐曲传美妙，无声胜有声；
因此，柔情的风笛，你尽情地吹；
无声的小曲不是吹给肉耳听的，
而是与更钟爱的人两心相期。
那树下的美少年歌永不歇，
那树上的绿叶也永不凋零，
大胆的恋人也永远吻不到她，

虽然离目的还差一步——但你也别生悲切；
虽然你还没有吻她的福气，但她永远不会老，
你的爱永恒，她的美永恒！

呵，幸福的树木！你的枝叶
不会剥落，从不曾离开春天；
琴师也有幸，精力永旺盛，
吹奏万古常新的乐曲；
呵，更为幸福的爱情，格外幸福的爱情！
永远温暖，令人欢慰，
永远激情，永远年轻；
这爱情超越了人间的爱情；
那人间的爱情让人生厌，叫人伤心，
让人额头发烫，焦灼人的舌根。

这些献祭的人是谁？
哦，神秘的祭司，走上神圣的祭坛，
这头小母牛披彩缎，饰花环，
对着苍天哞哞叫喊，啊，
是从哪个傍河傍海的小镇，
或哪个静静的堡寨山村，
来了这些人，在这虔诚的清晨？
呵，小镇，你的街道永远恬静；
没有一个人能赶回来，告诉你
为什么你是这样荒凉静寂。

啊，形状高雅！姿态美好！

上面细刻着大理石的男女之像，

那画图里头上有树枝、脚下有青草，

你嘲笑得我们不知如何是好，您这无言的形状，

就像“永恒”嘲笑我们一样；你这苍凉的田园风光！

当衰老把我们这代人消磨殆尽，

你仍留在下一代更痛苦的人之中，

你对他们说，你是人类的友人，

“美即是真，真即是美”这就包括

在这世界上，我们所知和需知的一切。

实战提升
Practising & Exercise

背景知识

约翰 · 济慈（John Keats），出生于 18 世纪末的伦敦，他是杰出的英诗作家之一，也是浪漫派的主要成员。济慈诗才横溢，与雪莱、拜伦齐名。他只活了 25 岁，但其遗下的诗篇一直誉满人间，被认为完美地体现了西方浪漫主义诗歌的特色，并被推崇为欧洲浪漫主义运动的杰出代表。他主张“美即是真，真即是美”（Beauty is truth, truth beauty），擅长描绘自然景色和事物外貌，表现景物的色彩感和立体感，重视写作技巧，语言追求华美，对后世抒情诗的创作影响极大。

在这首诗里，诗人把古瓮给他的一些感性的、富有生命力的、色彩斑斓的印象，通过他的神思妙想、艺术的提炼，把触及他灵魂的东西至美地表达了出来。昔日的生命不复存在，但生命不一定要依附于肉体，曾几何时，他们在古代雕刻家手中获得了“再生”，化为永恒之美长存人间，且超然于人间苦海的变幻，抚慰凄风苦雨中忧伤的心——美即是真，真即是美，此美乃不朽！故痛苦有限的生命可以在美和真中找到慰藉。整首诗在咏物过程中向我们提示了这样一个真理：人生短促、艺术长久！

单词注解

sylvan ['silvən] 森林的；多树木的

timbrel ['timbrəl] 铃鼓

adieu [ə'dju:] 告别，辞行

heifer ['hefə] 小母牛

maiden ['meidn] 少女

名句诵读

Though winning near the goal—yet，do not grieve；She cannot fade，though thou hast not thy bliss，Forever wilt thou love，and she be fair!

“Beauty is truth，truth beauty，” —that is all Ye know on earth，and all ye need to know.

Kubla Khan

Samuel Taylor Coleridge

In Xanadu did Kubla Khan
A stately pleasure **dome** *decree:*
Where Alph, the sacred river, ran
Through caverns measureless to man
Down to a sunless sea.
So twice five miles of **fertile** ground
With walls and towers were girdled round:
And there were gardens bright with sinuous rills
Where blossomed many an incense-bearing tree;
And here were forests ancient as the hills,
Enfolding sunny spots of greenery.

But oh! that deep romantic chasm which slanted
Down the green hill athwart a cedarn cover!
A savage place. as holy and enchanted
As e'er beneath a waning moon was haunted
By woman wailing for her **demon** *lover.*
And from this chasm, with ceaseless turmoil seething,
As if this earth in fast thick pants were breathing,
A mighty fountain momently was forced:

Amid whose sift half-intermitted burst
Huge fragments vaulted like rebounding hail,
Or chaffy grain beneath the thresher's flail:
And 'mid these dancing rocks at once and ever
It flung up momently the sacred river.
Five miles meandering with a mazy motion
Through wood and dale the sacred river ran,
Then reached the caverns measureless to man,
And sank in tumult to a lifless ocean:
And 'mid this tumult Kubla heard from far
Ancestral voices prophesying war!
The shadow of the dome of pleasure
Floated midway on the waves;
Where was heard the mingled measure
From the fountain and the caves.
It was a miracle of rare device,
A sunny pleasure dome with caves of ice!
A damsel with a dulcimer
In a vision once I saw:
It was an Abyssinian maid,
And on her dulcimer she played,
Singing of Mount Abora.
Could I revive within me
Her symphony and song,
To such a deep delight would win me,
That with music loud and long,
I would build that dome in air,
That sunny dome! those caves of ice!
And all who heard should see them there,

And all should cry, Beware! Beware!
His flashing eyes, his floating hair!
Weave a circle round him thrice,
And colse your eyes with holy dread,
For he on **honeydew** hath fed,
And drunk the milk of Paradise.

忽必烈汗

塞缪尔 · 泰勒 · 柯勒律治

忽必烈在上都颁了一道昭书:
建一座堂皇奢华的欢乐宫。
这地方有圣河亚佛流奔,
那宫殿多洞穴难测其底。
那河流流到海深暗蒙迷。
那皇官占土地方圆十里,
四周围上楼塔和城墙:
那里有花园,蜿蜒的溪河在其间闪耀,
园里树枝上鲜花盛开,一片芬芳;
御园内树参天与山同古,
树林间草如茵阳光充足。

那园间有深谷浩渺玄妙,
沿青山跨松林斜插远岙。
蛮荒地显神圣久具魅力,
恰似那微月下有女出没,
此女子为她的魔鬼情郎而凄声嚎哭!
有巨泉自深谷喷涌而出,

似乎这土地正喘息在快速而猛烈的悸动中，
又恰似急呼吸苍茫大地。
那飞瀑喷涌间时续时断，
夹带着大碎石如冰雹乱窜，
或者像打稻人连枷下一撮撮新稻；
在这些舞蹈的碎石中间，
迸发出那条神圣的溪河。
五里路蜿蜒流入迷宫，
穿森林越深谷水流淙淙，
于是到达了深不可测的洞门，
到最后带咆哮流入无声息的海中。
咆哮中忽必烈侧耳聆听，
遥远处诸远祖预示战争！
欢乐宫有倒影
宛在水波的中央漂动；
这儿能听到泉声与洞穴和谐的音韵，
让人听得真真切切。
此宫设计得颇具天工，
阳光灿烂的欢乐宫，连同那雪窟冰窖！
幻觉中我曾看见
弹古琴的一丽媛。
她来自东非海岸，
口唱阿巴拉山歌，
手挥古老的五弦。
她的容颜与歌曲都已飘逝，
我如果能忆起，

我将会大欣喜。

以至于我要用音乐高朗而又长久，

我能在空中建楼阁。

建起那朝阳宫，还有那雪窟冰窖！

听音乐的人都能看见，

他们全都会喊：当心！当心！

他，发彩飘飞，双眼如电！

赶紧绕他转三圈，

心带神圣畏惧闭上了双眼，

他以天国琼浆为饮，

以天国甘露为餐。

背景知识

塞缪尔·泰勒·柯勒律治（Samuel Taylor Coleridge），英国诗人和评论家，他的诗以其想像奇特，扑朔迷离，并追求象征、虚幻的哥特式风格与中古风格而著称。他一生是在贫病交困和鸦片成瘾的阴影下度过的，诗歌作品相对较少。尽管存在这些不利因素，柯勒律治还是坚持创作，确立了其在幻想浪漫诗歌方面的主要浪漫派诗人地位。

这首《忽必烈汗》是柯勒律治的代表作之一，是在一次服用鸦片后睡梦中所做的一首足有二三百行的长诗，无奈醒后由于客人来访，作者仅记下五十四行。尽管如此，仍堪称为诗坛一绝。此诗虚实结合，着重描写诗人梦境中的朦胧幻景，意象奇特，注重对比与比喻，尤其以其音乐性的韵律和丰富的修辞见长，是为一首不朽的世界名诗。

单词注解

dome [dəum] 穹窿；苍穹
fertile ['fə:tail] 富饶的，丰产的
demon ['di:mən] 恶魔，恶鬼
honeydew ['hʌnidju:] 甘露

名句诵读

In Xanadu did Kubla Khan A stately pleasure dome decree：Where Alph，the sacred river，ran Through caverns measureless to man Down to a sunless sea.

But oh! that deep romantic chasm which slanted Down the green hill athwart a cedarn cover! A savage place. as holy and enchanted As e'er beneath a waning moon was haunted By woman wailing for her demon lover.

It was a miracle of rare device，A sunny pleasure dome with caves of ice!

After Apple-Picking

Robert Frost

My long two-pointed **ladder's** *sticking through a tree*
Toward heaven still,
And there's a barrel that I didn't fill
Beside it, and there may be two or three
Apples I didn't pick upon some **bough**.
But I am done with apple-picking now.
Essence of winter sleep is on the night,
The scent of apples: I am drowsing off.
I cannot rub the strangeness from my sight
I got from looking through a pane of glass
I skimmed this morning from the drinking trough
And held against the world of hoary grass.
It melted, and I let it fall and break.
But I was well
Upon my way to sleep before it fell,
And I could tell
What form my dreaming was about to take.
Magnified apples appear and disappear,
Stem end and blossom end
And every fleck of russet showing clear.

My instep arch not only keeps the ache,
It keeps the pressure of a ladder-round.
I feel the ladder sway as the boughs bend.
And I keep hearing from the cellar bin
The rumbling sound
Of load on load of apples coming in.
For I have had too much
Of apple-picking： I am overtired
Of the great harvest I myself desired.
There were ten thousand thousand fruit to touch,
Cherish in hand，lift down，and not let fall.
For all
That struck the earth,
No matter if not bruised or spiked with stubble,
Went surely to the cider-apple heap
As of no worth.
One can see what will trouble
This sleep of mine，whatever sleep it is.
Were he not gone,
The woodchuck could say whether it's like his
Long sleep，as I describe its coming on,
Or just some human sleep.

摘苹果后

罗伯特·弗洛斯特

我那长梯穿过一棵苹果树，
朝上指着天，
树旁的苹果筐我还未摘满，
可能还有两三个苹果
还留在枝头。
但摘苹果这活儿算告一段落了
夜晚已经弥漫着冬眠的气息，
那苹果的香气已催我入眠。
我揉揉眼睛，
却揉不掉眼前的奇怪，
这怪景像来自今天早晨，
我从饮水槽里揭起一层冰，
像一块窗玻璃，隔窗望向
一个草枯霜重的世界。
冰融了，我由它掉下、碎掉。
可是没等它落地，我就
快进入梦乡了。
我能告诉你
我的梦以何种形式呈现。

放大的苹果出现又消逝，
蒂端花脐
和每个赤褐色斑都能看见。
我的弓形脚背不但保持着弓形，
而且让梯子在压力下平衡。
我感觉到树枝弯下时梯子摇摆。
我不断地听到从酒窖苹果筐里
传出了倒苹果的
摩擦声。
因为我摘苹果摘得
太多：我已为
自己希望的大丰收弄得疲惫不堪。
有千千万万个苹果要你去摘去摸，
得轻轻地去拿，轻轻地放，
不能往地上掉。只要一掉地，
所有苹果，
不管有没有摔破，还是插上了什么茬儿，
都会因此失去价值
而扔到造酒的苹果堆里。
你们会明白什么会扰乱
我的睡眠，不管我怎么个睡法。
如果土拨鼠没有走开，
听我讲睡梦怎样来到我的身边，
那它就可以说，
这跟它的冬眠倒有些像，
或者说，这不过是人类的冬眠。

实战提升
Practising & Exercise

背景知识

罗伯特 · 弗洛斯特（Robert Frost），美国著名诗人。他堪称是 20 世纪 90 年代最受欢迎的诗人之一，他的一生取得了很大的成就：四次荣获普利策奖；被称为美国非官方的桂冠诗人；并在 1961 年肯尼迪总统就职典礼上被邀请朗诵其诗歌。弗罗斯特是一个生活在现代的传统诗人。其诗的形式和韵律都是严格按照传统的规则进行创作的，因而被称为“交替性诗人”。

这是一首典型的田园诗歌，写的就是一个果农果园辛苦收获他丰收的苹果。这首诗看似一首简单的叙事诗，可其中蕴涵着深刻的哲理和寓意。从接受美学（Receptional Aesthetic）的角度来看，每个人观赏的角度不同，其对其诗的理解也不尽相同。

单词注解

ladder ['lædə] 梯子
bough [bau] 大树枝
magnified ['mægnfaid] 放大的

名句诵读

My long two-pointed ladder's sticking through a tree Toward heaven still, And there's a barrel that I didn't fill Beside it, and there may be two or three Apples I didn't pick upon some bough.

I cannot rub the strangeness from my sight I got from looking through a pane of glass I skimmed this morning from the drinking trough And held against the world of hoary grass.

Were he not gone, The woodchuck could say whether it's like his Long sleep, as I describe its coming on, Or just some human sleep.

Death, Be Not Proud

John Donne

Death, be not proud, though some have called thee
Mighty and dreadful, for **thou** *art not so;*
For those whom thou think'st thou dost overthrow
Die not, poor Death, nor yet canst thou kill me.
From rest and sleep, which but thy pictures be,
Much pleasure; then from thee much more must flow,
And soonest our best men with thee do go,
Rest of their bones, and soul's delivery.
Thou art slave to fate, chance, kings, and **desperate** men,
And dost with poison, war, and sickness **dwell**,
And poppy or charms can make us sleep as well
And better than thy stroke; why swell'st thou then?
One short sleep past, we wake eternally
And death shall be no more; Death, thou shalt die.

死神，休得狂妄

约翰·邓恩

死神，你休得狂妄，尽管有人说你
如何强大，如何可怕，你并不是这样；
你以为你把谁打倒了，其实，
可怜的死神，他们没死；你现在也还杀不死我。
休息、睡眠，这些不过是你的写照，
既能给人享受，那你本人提供的一定更多；
我们最美好的人随你去得越早，
越能早日获得身体的休息，灵魂的解脱。
你是命运、机会、君主、亡命徒的奴隶，
你和毒药、战争、疾病同住在一起，
鸦片和咒符和你的打击相比，同样，
甚至更能催我入睡；那你何必趾高气扬呢？
睡了一小觉之后，我们便永远觉醒了，
再也不会有死亡，你死神也将死去。

实战提升
Practising & Exercise

背景知识

约翰 · 邓恩 (John Donne)，英国著名诗人、牧师。他的作品中显示出了现实和感性的风格，包括十四行诗、爱情诗、宗教诗、警句、挽歌、歌曲、讽刺和说教。

这首诗选自约翰 · 邓恩的《神圣十四行诗》。死亡对诗人来说仅仅意味着休憩和睡眠，意味着灵魂的解脱。在他的心中，死神是“命运、机会、君主和亡命徒的奴隶”，死神和罪恶同居在一起，死神也总有死亡的那一天。所以，诗人对死神极为蔑视，也表达了自己对死亡毫不畏惧的心态。

单词注解

thou [θau]【古】汝，尔，你

desperate ['despərit] 危急的；绝望的

dwell [dwel] 居住，住

名句诵读

Death，be not proud，though some have called thee Mighty and dreadful，for thou art not so；For those whom thou think'st thou dost overthrow Die not，poor Death，nor yet canst thou kill me.

From rest and sleep，which but thy pictures be，Much pleasure；then from thee much more must flow，And soonest our best men with thee do go，Rest of their bones，and soul's delivery.

One short sleep past，we wake eternally And death shall be no more；Death，thou shalt die.

Old Black Joe

Stephen Collins Foster

1

Gone are the days when my heart was young and gay;
Gone are my friends from the **cotton** *fields away;*
Gone from the earth to a better land I know,
I hear their **gentle** *voices calling,*
"Old Black Joe!"
I'm coming, I'm coming, for my head is bending low;
I hear their gentle voices calling,
"Old Black Joe!"

2

Why do I weep when my heart should feel no pain?
Why do I sigh that my friends come not again?
Grieving for forms now departed **long** *ago,*
I hear their gentle voices calling,
"Old Black Joe!"

3

Where are thee hearts once so happy and so free?

The children so dear that I held upon my knee?

Gone to the shore where my ***soul*** *has longed to go,*

I hear their gentle voices calling,

"Old Black Joe!"

老黑乔

史蒂芬·柯林斯·福斯特

1

快乐童年，如今一去不复返，
亲爱的朋友，都已离开家园，
离开尘世到那天上的乐园，
我听见他们轻声把我呼唤，
“老黑乔！”
我来了，我来了，
我已年老背又弯，
我听见他们轻声把我呼唤。

2

为何哭泣，如今我不应忧伤？
为何叹息，朋友不能重相见？
为何悲痛，亲人去世已多年。
我听见他们轻声把我呼唤，
“老黑乔！”

3

昔日快乐无羁的人们，如今安在?

还有，我抱在膝上可爱的小家伙?

他们都已经到了我灵魂所渴望去的海岸，

我听见他们柔声呼唤，

“老黑乔！”

背景知识

史蒂芬 · 柯林斯 · 福斯特 (Stephen Collins Foster)，美国作曲家。他生于匹兹堡东边的一个小镇，在家中十个兄弟姊妹中排行第九。因为家中并不富裕，所以自小几乎失学在家，但他喜欢阅读及热爱音乐。青少年时期与哥哥等合组一个音乐社，名为“方桌武士”，在其十八岁时写下其生平第一首歌《打开窗扉的爱》。

这是一首由斯蒂芬 · 福斯特作词作曲，在美国特别是在美国黑人中广为流传的歌曲。歌中向世人倾诉了黑人兄弟辛劳艰难最终将走向天堂与家人团聚的一生。这首歌反映了一个老黑奴痛苦的一生和回忆。如今老黑奴年事已高，沧桑岁月压弯了腰，他将走向理想的乐园。他的身边时时响起“他们轻声的呼唤”。这呼唤是心灵的呼唤，这呼唤将把他带入天堂和在那里的亲人们团圆。

单词注解

cotton ['kɔtn] 棉，棉花
gentle ['dʒentl] 温和的；和善的
long [lɔŋ] 渴望
soul [səul] 灵魂，心灵

名句诵读

Gone are the days when my heart was young and gay；Gone are my friends from the cotton fields away；Gone from the earth to a better land I know，I hear their gentle voices calling，“Old Black Joe!”

Why do I weep when my heart should feel no pain? Why do I sigh that my friends come not again? Grieving for forms now departed long ago，I hear their gentle voices calling，“Old Black Joe!”

Where are thee hearts once so happy and so free? The children so dear that I held upon my knee? Gone to the shore where my soul has longed to go，I hear their gentle voices calling，“Old Black Joe!”

I Hear America Singing

Walt Whitman

I Hear America singing, the varied ***carols*** *I hear.*
Those of mechanics, each one singing his as it should be blithe and strong,
The carpenter singing his as he measures his plank or beam,
The mason singing his as he makes ready for work, or leaves off work,
The boatman singing what belongs to him in his boat, the deckhand singing on the steamboat deck,
The shoemaker singing as he sits on his bench, the **hatter** singing as he stands,
The wood-cutter's song, the ploughboy's, on his way in the morning, or at the noon intermission or at sundown,
The delicious singing of the mother, or of the young wife at work, or of the girl sewing or washing, Each singing what belongs to her and to none else,
The day what belongs to the day—At night, the party of young fellows, robust, friendly,
Singing with open mouths their strong ***melodious*** *songs.*

我听见美洲在歌唱

沃尔特 · 惠特曼

我听见美国在唱歌，我听到了各种颂歌，
机械工人在歌唱着，每个人都在唱着他那快乐而嘹亮的歌，
木匠边丈量着他的木板和房梁，边唱着他的歌，
瓦匠在工作或休息的时候唱着他的歌，
船夫歌唱着他船上的一切，水手也在轮船的甲板上歌唱着，
鞋匠坐在板凳上歌唱，帽匠也在站着歌唱，
伐木者、耕童们走在清晨的路上，在歇息的中午，
或在日落时分歌唱着，
我还听到来自母亲的美妙歌声，正在操作的年轻的
妻子们或缝衣或洗衣女孩子们的歌。
每个人歌唱属于他或她而不属于别人的一切，
白天唱着属于白天的歌，夜晚，在这一群体格健壮、友好相处
的年轻人聚会上，
唱着他们那嘹亮而优美的旋律。

背景知识

沃尔特 · 惠特曼（Walt Whitman），美国诗人。他一生的诗作都被收在《草叶集》里了。在这部不断扩充再版的诗集里，诗人以主人翁的姿态，以高亢的声调，歌颂了他先进的国家、普通的人民群众、富于民主和自由传统的民族精神。

该诗作于林肯被刺后不久，直到现在，美洲的男女老少，皆能朗诵。那些衣帽商人也以“我听见美洲在歌唱”一诗为时髦，把这句诗作为商标，订在衣领上、帽沿边。人们都纷纷去购买标有“我听见美洲在歌唱”诗句的衣帽。

单词注解

carol ['kærəl]（圣诞）颂歌；赞美诗
blithe [blaið] 无忧无虑的；漫不经心的
hatter ['hætə] 帽商
melodious [mi'ləudjəs] 旋律优美的，悦耳动听的

名句诵读

I Hear America singing，the varied carols I hear.

The delicious singing of the mother，or of the young wife at work，or of the girl sewing or washing，Each singing what belongs to her and to none else，The day what belongs to the day—At night，the party of young fellows，robust，friendly，Singing with open mouths their strong melodious songs.

Sadness of August

Lin Huiyin

*In a yellow **pond** there are white ducks swimming.*
*Only a little taller than people, **sorghums** are still green.*
Where should I put, in this pounding heart,
A narrow path in the field, this sadness in August.

Rain washed the sky clean last night, sun shines
On hills and leaves some shadows,
*Sheep follow the **shepherd** into the village,*
And shading a well, a big tree looks like a heart.

No one ever spoke of August, summer is over
And fall isn't here. I look onto a farmland
*And then at the **squashes** over the earth wall,*
I just don't understand how life and dream connect.

八月的忧愁

林徽因

黄水塘里游着白鸭，
高粱梗油青的刚高过头，
这跳动的心怎样安插，
田里一窄条路，八月里这忧愁？

天是昨夜雨洗过的，山岗
照着太阳又留一片影；
羊跟着放羊的转进村庄，
一大棵树荫下罩着井，又像是心！

从没有人说过八月什么话，
夏天过去了，也不到秋天。
但我望着田垄，土墙上的瓜，
仍不明白生活同梦怎样的连牵。

背景知识

林徽因 (1904~1955)，福建闽侯人。林徽因是中国著名的建筑学家和作家，也是中国第一位女性建筑学家，被胡适誉为中国一代才女。30 年代初，与夫婿梁思成用现代科学方法研究中国古代建筑，成为这个学术领域的开拓者，后来在这方面获得了巨大的学术成就。在中国现代女作家中，林徽因是极有天分、极具个性、极为独特的一位，她在建筑学上的卓越成就也一直为研究者所关注的话题，深受后人尊敬。

在这首诗中，诗人通过营造水塘白鸭、山岗村庄、田垄土墙等充满古朴、清幽、静雅情趣的意象，流露出其自身对自然景致的迷醉与悟感，使诗歌映现出反璞归真的诗情画意。可以说，林徽因抒写自然美的诗作相比较其他作家而言呈现出了一种本真而从容的别样风味。诗歌的语言凝练、含蓄、整饬，富有韵律感和节奏感。

单词注解

pond [pɔnd] 池塘
sorghum ['sɔ:gəm]【植】高粱，蜀黍
shepherd ['ʃepəd] 牧羊人
squash [skwɔʃ] 挤压；硬塞

名句诵读

In a yellow pond there are white ducks swimming.
Only a little taller than people，sorghums are still green.

Rain washed the sky clean last night，sun shines On hills and leaves some shadows，Sheep follow the shepherd into the village，And shading a well，a big tree looks like a heart.

No one ever spoke of August，summer is over And fall isn't here. I look onto a farmland And then at the squashes over the earth wall，I just don't understand how life and dream connect.

Sun of the Sleepless

George Gordon Byron

*Sun of the sleepless! **melancholy** star!*
*Whose tearful beam glows **tremulously** far,*
That show'st the darkness thou canst not dispel,
How like art thou to joy remember'd well!

So gleams the past, the light of other days,
Which shines, but warms not with its powerless rays;
*A night-beam Sorrow watcheth to **behold**,*
Distinct but distant —clear—but, oh how cold!

失眠人的太阳

乔治·戈登·拜伦

呵，失眠人的太阳！忧郁的星！
有如泪珠，你射来抖颤的光明
只不过显现你逐不开的幽暗，
你多么像欢乐追忆在心坎！

“过去”，那往日的明辉也在闪烁，
但它微弱的光却没有一丝热；
“忧伤”尽在了望黑夜的一线光明，
它清晰，却遥远；灿烂，却多么寒冷！

背景知识

乔治·戈登·拜伦(George Gordon Byron)，19世纪英国伟大的浪漫主义诗人。他因对英国反动统治阶级的抨击而被迫长期离开祖国。他同情和支持欧洲各国的资产阶级民主革命和民族解放斗争，曾亲身参加意大利烧炭党人的革命活动，参加希腊人民反抗土耳其奴役的武装斗争，最后并以身殉。他的诗歌里塑造了一批"拜伦式英雄"，他们孤傲、狂热、浪漫，却充满了反抗精神，他们内心充满了孤独与苦闷，却又蔑视群小。恰尔德·哈罗德是拜伦诗歌中第一个"拜伦式英雄"。拜伦诗中最具有代表性、战斗性，也是最辉煌的作品是他的长诗《唐璜》。

单词注解

melancholy ['melənkəli] 忧郁；忧思
tremulously ['tremjuləs] 发抖地；畏惧地
behold [bi'həuld] 看；看见

名句诵读

Sun of the sleepless! melancholy star! Whose tearful beam glows tremulously far, That show'st the darkness thou canst not dispel, How like art thou to joy remember'd well!

So gleams the past, the light of other days, Which shines, but warms not with its powerless rays; .A night-beam Sorrow watcheth to behold, Distinct but distant —clear— but, oh how cold!

Wild Fire

Ai Qing

Set these black nights **ablaze**
On these lofty mountaintops
Extend your arms of flame
Embrace her dark-blue, ice-cold **bosom**
From the tips of your high-leaping flames
Let your sparks fly out
Let them descend, like a host of sprites
Down the unfathomable, dark-cold abyss
Let them flash on the souls fast asleep there
Let them, even if only in dazed dreaming
Dance, for once, the dance of joy.

Set these black nights ablaze
Lat the flames climb higher and higher!
Let your **joyous** configurations
Rise from the ground to the heavens
Inspire this wearisome world of ours
With the dance of your spirited fire
Rise up and soar!
Let the thousand eyes of this dark night

Look to you

Let the hearts on this dark night

All heed your earth-shaking summons

Oh，your Joyous flames

Oh，your trembling flames

Listen! From what profound corner

Comes this song that **hymns** *your praise like a waterfall...*

野　火

艾　青

在这些黑夜里燃烧起来
在这些高高的山巅上
伸出你的光焰的手
去抚扪夜的宽阔的胸脯
去抚扪深蓝的冰凉的胸脯
从你的最高处跳动着的尖顶
把你的火星飞飏起来
让它们像群仙似的飘落在
寻些莫测的黑暗而又冰冷的深谷
去照见那些沉睡的灵魂
让它们即使在缥缈的梦中
也能得一次狂欢的舞蹈

在这些黑夜燃烧起来
更高些！更高些！
让你的欢乐的形体
从地面升向高空
使我们这困倦的世界

因了你的火光的鼓舞
苏醒起来！喧腾起来！
让这黑夜里的一切的眼
都在看望着你
让这黑夜里的一切的心
都因了你的召唤而震荡
欢笑的火焰啊
颤动的火焰啊

听呀从什么深邃的角落
传来了那赞颂你的瀑布似的歌声……

背景知识

艾青（1910 ~ 1996），现代诗人，原名蒋海澄。在中国新诗发展史上，艾青是继郭沫若、闻一多等人之后又一位推动一代诗风、并产生过重要影响的诗人，在世界上也享有声誉。他在 1985 年，曾获法国文学艺术最高勋章，这是我国诗人得到的第一个国外文学艺术的最高级大奖。其诗作《我爱这土地》被选入人教版中学语文教材。艾青早期的诗歌咏叹民族命运，呈现出忧郁、感伤逐渐转向悲壮、高昂的诗风。在诗学上受凡尔哈仑等外国现代诗人的影响。50 年代他直接表现新生活及建设者的诗作，疏离已有的艺术个性，显得平淡，但保持着原有诗思的格局。70 年代末复出后，他诗思如涌，精心构撰大量的诗歌，主题接续三四十年代渴求光明、真理的情思线索，并有大幅度延伸，更为深沉、凝重、睿智，注重在具体物象中把握超越物象的意蕴，走向象征。

单词注解

ablaze [ə'bleiz] 着火，起火
bosom ['buzəm] 胸；怀
joyous ['dʒɔiəs] 快乐的；高兴的
hymn [him] 赞美诗，圣歌

名句诵读

Set these black nights ablaze On these lofty mountaintops Extend your arms of flame Embrace her dark-blue，ice-cold bosom From the tips of your high-leaping flames Let your sparks fly out Let them descend，like a host of sprites Down the unfathomable，dark-cold abyss Let them flash on the souls fast asleep there Let them，even if only in dazed dreaming Dance，for once，the dance of joy.

Listen! From what profound corner Comes this song that hymns your praise like a waterfall...

Twenty–Four Years

Dylan Thomas

Twenty–four years remind the tears of my eyes.
(Bury the dead for fear that they walk to the grave in labour.)
In the groin of the natural doorway I crouched like a ***tailor***
Sewing a ***shroud*** *for a journey*
By the light of the meat–eating sun.
Dressed to die, the sensual ***strut*** *begun,*
With my red ***veins*** *full of money,*
In the final direction of the ***elementary*** *town*
I advance for as long as forever is.

二十四年

狄兰 · 托马斯

回顾二十四年的岁月，我的眼里充满泪水。
（埋葬死者以免他们在阵痛中步向坟地。）
我曾蹲在天然门廊的腹沟里，
像个裁缝，借用吞食一切的阳光，
缝制一件旅行用的寿衣。
盛装就死，肉欲之徜徉已开始，
我的红色血管里满是金钱，
朝着小市镇最后的方向
我永久地前行。

背景知识

狄兰 · 托马斯（Dylan Thomas），二十世纪最具影响力的英语诗人之一。虽然狄兰主要是位诗人，他也创作过电影剧本和短篇小说。在他刚庆祝完39岁生日后不久，死于醉酒。狄兰 · 托马斯的诗歌围绕生、欲、死三大主题；诗风粗犷而热烈，音韵充满活力而不失严谨；其肆意设置的密集意象相互撞击、相互制约，表现自然的生长力和人性的律动。狄兰 · 托马斯的诗歌掀开了英美诗歌史上的新的篇章。

单词注解

tailor ['teilə] 裁缝师；服装店
shroud [ʃraud] 寿衣，裹尸布
strut [strʌt] 高视阔步；趾高气扬地走
vein [vein] 静脉，血管
elementary [ˌeli'mentəri] 初级的，基础的

名句诵读

Twenty-four years remind the tears of my eyes.

In the groin of the natural doorway I crouched like a tailor Sewing a shroud for a journey By the light of the meat-eating sun.

Dressed to die, the sensual strut begun, With my red veins full of money, In the final direction of the elementary town I advance for as long as forever is.

Hope

Emily Bronte

Hope was but a timid friend;
She sat without the grated **den,**
Watching how my fate would tend,
Even as selfish-hearted men.

She was cruel in her fear;
Through the bars one weary day,
I looked out to see her there,
And she turned her face away!

Like a false ***guard***, *false watch keeping,*
Still in strife, she whispered peace;
She would sing while I was weeping,
If I listened, she would cease.

False she was, and unrelenting;
When my last joys **strewed** the ground,
Even Sorrow saw, repenting,
Those sad relics scattered round;

Hope，whose whisper would have given
Balm to all my ***frenzied*** *pain.,*
Stretched her wings，and soared to heaven，
Went，and ne’er returned again!

希　望

艾米莉·勃朗特

希望只是个羞怯的友伴。
她坐在我的囚牢之外，
以自私者的冷眼旁观
观察我的命运的好歹。

她因胆怯而如此冷酷。
郁闷的一天，我透过铁栏，
想看到我的希望的面目，
却见她立即背转了脸！

像一个假看守在假意监视，
一面敌对一面又暗示和平；
当我哀泣时她吟唱歌词，
当我静听她却噤口无声。

她心如铁石而且虚假。
当我最后的欢乐落满地，
见此悲惨的遗物四处抛撒，

就连“哀愁”也遗憾不已；

而希望，她本来能悄悄耳语
为痛苦欲狂者搽膏止痛，
却伸展双翼向天堂飞去，
一去不回，从此不见影踪。

背景知识

艾米莉 · 勃朗特（Emily Bronte），英国著名女作家，《呼啸山庄》是她的代表作。她曾与姐妹合出过一本诗集，直到 20 世纪她才被公认为英国三大女诗人之一。艾米莉生性内向而孤傲，深居简出，喜欢一个人在荒原上散步。长相平平的她一辈子都没有谈过恋爱。与她的姊妹一样，艾米莉的身体因为当地的气候而显得衰弱。在 1848 年 9 月她的兄弟的丧礼期间，艾米莉感染了风寒，并且拒绝服用药物。1848 年 12 月 19 日，艾米莉因结核病去世。

单词注解

den [den] 洞穴，窝巢
guard [gɑ:d] 哨兵；卫兵；警备员
strew [stru:] 铺盖；点缀
frenzied ['frenzid] 狂乱的；疯狂（似）的

名句诵读

Hope was but a timid friend；She sat without the grated den，Watching how my fate would tend，Even as selfish-hearted men.

Like a false guard，false watch keeping，Still in strife，she whispered peace；She would sing while I was weeping，If I listened，she would cease.

Hope，whose whisper would have given Balm to all my frenzied pain，Stretched her wings，and soared to heaven，Went，and ne' er returned again!

………… Goodbye Again，Cambridge …………

再别康桥

Down by the Salley Gardens

William Butler Yeats

Down by the salley gardens my love and I did meet;
She passed the salley gardens with little snow-white feet.
She **bid** me take love easy, as the leaves grow on the tree;
But I, being young and foolish, with her would not agree.
In a field by the river my love and I did stand,
And on my leaning shoulder she laid her **snow-white** *hand.*
She bid me take life easy, as the grass grows on the **weirs**;
But I was young and foolish, and now am full of tears.

来到柳园

威廉 · 巴特勒 · 叶芝

我与她赴幽会来到柳园，
她来时足娇小色白如棉。
听她讲爱莫急如叶慢长，
那时候小而蠢，和她意见不一
我与她站立在河边田野，
她雪白的手倚在我肩。
听她讲生活像水草慢长，
那时候小而蠢，如今空把泪洒。

背景知识

威廉 · 巴特勒 · 叶芝 (William Butler Yeats)，爱尔兰诗人、剧作家，著名的神秘主义者。叶芝是“爱尔兰文艺复兴运动”的领袖，也是艾比剧院 (Abbey Theatre) 的创建者之一。1865 年 6 月 13 日出生于都柏林。曾在都柏林大都会美术学院学习绘画，1887 年开始专门从事诗歌创作，被诗人艾略特誉为“当代最伟大的诗人”。

这首诗也被译为《莎莉花园》，在时态的运用上也有独特之处。全诗除了最后半行用现在时态以外都是过去时态。这说明过去对人们的现在具有十分重要的意义。在诗的最后，诗人用一般现在时是意味深长的。虽然对现在情况的描述只有五个词便戛然而止，但是，由于诗人把这几个词放在全诗最突出的位置，所以给人意犹未尽的感觉。这首貌似简单的诗，却向人们揭示了生活的哲理：对待爱情和生活，人们应当顺其自然，就像“绿叶长在树枝上”，“青草长在河堰上”。不然，会因为一时的“愚蠢”而遗恨终生。

单词注解

bid [bid] 命令，吩咐
snow-white 雪白的；纯白的
weir [wiə] 堰；坝

名句诵读

Down by the salley gardens my love and I did meet; She passed the salley gardens with little snow-white feet.

In a field by the river my love and I did stand, And on my leaning shoulder she laid her snow-white hand. She bid me take life easy, as the grass grows on the weirs; But I was young and foolish, and now am full of tears.

Goodbye Again, Cambridge

Xu Zhimo

I leave softly, gently,
Exactly as I came.
I wave to the western sky,
Telling it goodbye softly, gently.

The golden willow at the river edge
Is the setting sun's bride.
Her **quivering** reflection
Stays fixed in my mind.

Green grass on the bank
Dances on a watery floor
In bright reflection.
I wish myself a bit of waterweed
Vibrating to the ripple. Of the River Cam.

That creek in the shade of the great elms
Is not a creek but a shattered rainbow, Printed on the water
And inlaid with duckweed, It is my lost dream.

Hunting a dream? Wielding a long punting pole
I get my boat into green water,
Into still greener grass.
In a flood of starlight，On a river of silver and diamond
I sing to my heart's content.

But，I cannot sing aloud
Quietness is my farewell music；
Even Summer insects heap silence for me
Silent is Cambridge tonight!

I leave quietly
As I came quietly.
Gently I **flick** *my sleeves*
Not even a wisp of cloud will I bring away.

再别康桥

徐志摩

轻轻的我走了，
正如我轻轻的来，
我轻轻的招手，
作别西天的云彩。

那河畔的金柳，
是夕阳中的新娘，
波光里的艳影，
在我的心头荡漾。

软泥上的青荇，
油油的在水底招摇；
在康河的柔波里，
我甘心作一条水草！

那榆荫下的一潭，
不是清泉，是天上虹；
揉碎在浮藻间，

沉淀着彩虹似的梦。

寻梦！撑一支长篙，
向青草更青处漫溯，
满载一船星辉，
在星辉斑斓里放歌。

但我不能放歌，
悄悄是别离的笙箫。
夏虫也为我沉默，
沉默是今晚的康桥！

悄悄的我走了，
正如我悄悄的来，
我挥一挥衣袖，
不带走一片云彩！

实战提升
Practising & Exercise

背景知识

徐志摩（1897 ~ 1931），现代诗人、散文家。徐志摩是新月派代表诗人，新月诗社成员。1921 年入剑桥大学，研究政治经济学。在剑桥两年深受西方教育的熏陶及欧美浪漫主义和唯美派诗人的影响。1931 年因飞机失事遇难。

这是一首优美的抒情诗，宛如一曲优雅动听的轻音乐。1928 年秋，作者再次到英国访问，旧地重游，勃发了诗兴，将自己的生活体验化作缕缕情思，融汇在所抒写的康桥美丽的景色里，也驰骋在诗人的想象之中。

单词注解

exactly [ig'zæktli] 确切地，精确地
quiver ['kwivə] 颤抖；发抖
vibrate [vai'breit] 颤动；振动
flick [flik] 轻打；轻弹

名句诵读

I leave softly, gently, Exactly as I came. I wave to the western sky, Telling it goodbye softly, gently.

Green grass on the bank Dances on a watery floor In bright reflection.

I leave quietly As I came quietly. Gently I flick my sleeves Not even a wisp of cloud will I bring away

背景知识

艾米莉·狄金森（Emily Dickinson），美国诗人。20岁开始写诗，早期的诗大都已散失，1858年后闭门不出，70年代后几乎不出房门，文学史上称她为“阿默斯特的女尼”。她的诗风凝炼，比喻尖新。她生前只出版过10首诗，默默无闻，死后近70年开始得到文学界的认真关注，被现代派诗人追认为先驱。与同时代的惠特曼，一同被奉为美国最伟大诗人。

单词注解

lapsed [læpst] 流失的
imperceptibly [ˌimpəˈseptəbl] 不可觉地
perfidy [ˈpəːfidi] 不诚实；背信弃义
distilled [disˈtild] 净化的
sequestered [siˈkwestəd] 僻静的；隐蔽的

名句诵读

The Summer lapsed away—Too imperceptible at last

A courteous，yet harrowing Grace，As Guest，that would be gone—

Our Summer made her light escape Into the Beautiful.

背景知识

徐志摩（1897 ~ 1931），现代诗人、散文家。徐志摩是新月派代表诗人，新月诗社成员。1921 年入剑桥大学，研究政治经济学。在剑桥两年深受西方教育的熏陶及欧美浪漫主义和唯美派诗人的影响。1931 年因飞机失事遇难。

这是一首优美的抒情诗，宛如一曲优雅动听的轻音乐。1928 年秋，作者再次到英国访问，旧地重游，勃发了诗兴，将自己的生活体验化作缕缕情思，融汇在所抒写的康桥美丽的景色里，也驰骋在诗人的想象之中。

单词注解

exactly [ig'zæktli] 确切地，精确地
quiver ['kwivə] 颤抖；发抖
vibrate [vai'breit] 颤动；振动
flick [flik] 轻打；轻弹

名句诵读

I leave softly，gently，Exactly as I came. I wave to the western sky，Telling it goodbye softly，gently.

Green grass on the bank Dances on a watery floor In bright reflection.

I leave quietly As I came quietly. Gently I flick my sleeves Not even a wisp of cloud will I bring away

As Imperceptibly as Grief

Emily Dickinson

The Summer ***lapsed*** *away—*
Too ***imperceptible*** *at last*
To seem like **Perfidy**—
A Quietness **distilled**
As Twilight long begun,
Or Nature spending with herself
Sequestered Afternoon—
The Dusk drew earlier in—
The Morning foreign shone—
A courteous, yet harrowing Grace,
As Guest, that would be gone—
And thus, without a Wing
Or service of a Keel
Our Summer made her light escape
Into the Beautiful.

夏之逃逸

艾米莉・狄金森

不知不觉地，有如忧伤，
夏日竟然消逝了，
如此的难以察觉，简直
不像是有意潜逃。
向晚的微光很早便开始，
沉淀出一片寂静，
不然便是消瘦的四野
将下午悄悄幽禁。
黄昏比往日来得更早，
清晨的光彩已陌生——
一种拘礼而恼人的风度，
像即欲离开的客人。
就像如此，也不用翅膀，
也不劳小舟相送，
我们的夏日悄悄逃去，
没入了美的境中。

背景知识

艾米莉 · 狄金森（Emily Dickinson），美国诗人。20岁开始写诗，早期的诗大都已散失，1858年后闭门不出，70年代后几乎不出房门，文学史上称她为“阿默斯特的女尼”。她的诗风凝炼，比喻尖新。她生前只出版过10首诗，默默无闻，死后近70年开始得到文学界的认真关注，被现代派诗人追认为先驱。与同时代的惠特曼，一同被奉为美国最伟大诗人。

单词注解

lapsed [læpst] 流失的
imperceptibly [ˌimpəˈseptəbl] 不可觉地
perfidy [ˈpəːfidi] 不诚实；背信弃义
distilled [disˈtild] 净化的
sequestered [siˈkwestəd] 僻静的；隐蔽的

名句诵读

The Summer lapsed away—Too imperceptible at last

A courteous，yet harrowing Grace，As Guest，that would be gone—

Our Summer made her light escape Into the Beautiful.

I Wandered Lonely as a Cloud

William Wordsworth

I wandered lonely as a cloud
That floats on high o'er vales and hills,
When all at once I saw a crowd,
A host, of golden **daffodils**;
Beside the lake, beneath the trees,
Fluttering and dancing in the **breeze**.

Continuous as the stars that shine
And twinkle on the milky way,
They stretched in never-ending line
Along the margin of a bay:
Ten thousand saw I at a glance,
Tossing their heads in **sprightly** dance.

The waves beside them danced; but they
Out-did the sparkling waves in glee:
A poet could not but be gay,
In such a jocund company:
I gazed—and gazed—but little thought
What wealth the show to me had brought:

For oft, when on my couch I lie

In vacant or in pensive mood,

They flash upon that inward eye

Which is the bliss of solitude;

And then my heart with pleasure fills,

And dances with the daffodils.

我如行云独自游

威廉 · 华兹华斯

我如行云独自游，
在河谷与群山之上飘浮，
蓦然间，我看到一大片
一大片，金黄的水仙；
在湖畔，在树下，
在微风中翩翩起舞。

连绵不断，像繁星闪亮，
闪烁在银河，
沿着水弯的边缘，
它们伸展成无穷无尽的行列；
我一眼便看到成千上万朵水仙，
欢蹦乱跳，点头晃脑。

他们身边的湖波也在舞动，
但花儿比闪亮的水波舞得更欢。
有这样欢乐的花们为伴，
诗客怎能不开心颜？

久看水仙未遑思，
此景竟成我才源。

当我躺在卧榻之上，
或者茫然，或者沉思，
此时水仙会闪现在我的心中，
这是孤寂中无上的幸福；
我心因此而倍感快乐，
与水仙翩然共舞。

背景知识

威廉 · 华兹华斯（William Wordsworth），英国浪漫主义诗人。华兹华斯诗歌创作的黄金时期在 1797 年到 1807 年。随着声誉逐渐上升，他的创作逐渐走向衰退。到了 1830 年，他的成就已得到普遍承认，1843 年被封为英国桂冠诗人。18 世纪末、19 世纪初在英国西北部的湖畔有一些诗人聚集，其诗作多描写湖区，故称他们为“湖畔派”。

这首诗可以分成两大部分；写景和抒情。诗的开篇以第一人称叙述，格调显得低沉忧郁。诗人一方面竭力捕捉回忆的渺茫信息，另一方面又觉得独自漂游，可以自由自在地欣赏大自然所赋予的美景。他把自己比作一朵流云，随意飘荡，富有想象的诗句暗示诗人有一种排遣孤独、向往自由的心情。在他的回忆中，水仙花缤纷茂密，如繁星点点在微风中轻盈飘舞。

单词注解

daffodil ['dæfədil] 水仙；水仙花

breeze [bri:z] 微风，和风

sprightly ['spraitli] 生气勃勃的；轻快的

jocund ['dʒɔkənd] 欢乐的，快活的，高兴的

bliss [blis] 极乐，至喜；天堂之乐

名句诵读

I wandered lonely as a cloud That floats on high o'er vales and hills，When all at once I saw a crowd，A host，of golden daffodils；Beside the lake，beneath the trees，Fluttering and dancing in the breeze.

For oft，when on my couch I lie In vacant or in pensive mood，They flash upon that inward eye Which is the bliss of solitude；And then my heart with pleasure fills，And dances with the daffodils.

Song of Nature

Ralph Waldo Emerson

Mine are the night and morning,
The pits of air, the gulf of space,
The sportive sun, the gibbous moon,
The ***innumerable*** *days.*

I hid in the solar glory,
I am dumb in the pealing song,
I rest on the pitch of the torrent,
In slumber I am strong.

No numbers have counted my tallies,
No tribes my house can fill,
I sit by the shining Fount of Life,
And pour the **deluge** still;

And ever by delicate powers
Gathering along the centuries
From race on race the rarest flowers,
My wreath shall nothing miss.

And many a thousand summers
My apples ripened well,
And light from meliorating stars
With firmer glory fell.

I wrote the past in characters
Of rock and fire the scroll,
The building in the coral sea,
The planting of the coal.

And thefts from satellites and rings
And broken stars I drew,
And out of spent and aged things
I formed the world anew;

What time the gods kept carnival,
Tricked out in star and flower,
And in cramp elf and saurian forms
They swathed their too much power.

Time and Thought were my surveyors,
They laid their courses well,
They boiled the sea, and baked the layers
Or granite, marl, and shell.

But he, the man-child glorious, —
Where tarries he the while?
The rainbow shines his harbinger,
The sunset gleams his smile.

My boreal lights leap upward,
Forthright my planets roll,
And still the man-child is not born,
The summit of the whole.

Must time and tide forever run?
Will never my winds go sleep in the west?
Will never my wheels which whirl the sun
And satellites have rest?

Too much of donning and doffing,
Too slow the rainbow fades,
I weary of my robe of snow,
My leaves and my cascades;

I tire of globes and races,
Too long the game is played;
What without him is summer's pomp,
Or winter's frozen shade?

I travail in pain for him,
My creatures travail and wait;
His couriers come by squadrons,
He comes not to the gate.

Twice I have moulded an image,
And thrice outstretched my hand,
Made one of day, and one of night,

And one of the salt sea–sand.

One in a Judaean manger,
And one by Avon stream,
One over against the mouths of Nile,
And one in the Academe.

I moulded kings and saviours,
And bards o'er kings to rule; —
But fell the starry influence short,
The cup was never full.

Yet whirl the glowing wheels once more,
And mix the bowl again;
Seethe, fate! the ancient elements,
Heat, cold, wet, dry, and peace, and pain.

Let war and trade and creeds and song
Blend, ripen race on race,
The sunburnt world a man shall breed
Of all the zones, and countless days.

No ray is dimmed, no atom worn,
My oldest force is good as new,
And the fresh rose on yonder thorn
Gives back the bending heavens in dew.

自然之歌

拉尔夫·瓦尔多·爱默生

我拥有黑夜与清晨，
大气的沟壑，空间的深渊，
太阳嬉闹，月华盈盈，
数不清的一天天。

我躲进阳光的辉煌，
在隆隆的歌里沉默，
停在洪流的波面，
我在酣眠中强壮。

没有数字将我计数，
没有部落充满我的房屋，
坐在波光潋滟的生命泉边，
我默默将洪流倾注；

曾经倚靠精妙的力量
沿着诸多的世纪采集
一种接一种珍稀的花朵，

我的花冠上什么都不会逃过。

经过成千上万个夏季
我的苹果都成熟了，
变化着的星星闪烁
撒下坚实的光芒。

我用岩石的质地书写往昔
并焚烧那些纸制卷轴，
珊瑚海中的建筑哦，
煤矿的基底。

从那些卫星和轨道间
我窃取毁坏的星宿，
用那些衰竭与老化之物
我将全新的世界构筑；

何时诸神流连于狂欢，
用星星和花朵妆扮，
也用痉挛的侏儒与蜥蜴标本
赋予过多的神力给它们。

时间与思想将我检验，
铺设它们美好的进程，
它们煮沸大海，烧硬岩层
或是花岗岩、泥灰岩和地壳。

而他，光荣的男孩，——
此时他在何处流连？
彩虹为他映出预言，
夕阳使他的微笑闪现。

我的北极光向上飞升，
我的行星都即刻开始运行，
那男孩，一切的顶点
却依然尚未出生，

时间与潮汐必将恒久运行？
我的风在西方永不入睡？
我那轮子转动太阳
和行星，永远都不会停？

太多的求取，太多的丢弃，
虹影太过缓慢地褪去，
我厌倦我那雪之长衣，
我的叶子和我的瀑流。

我厌倦众星及其运行，
这游戏已玩了太久；
没有他，怎一番夏日的盛景，
怎一番冬日冰冷的暗影？

我为他陷入劳苦伤痛，
我的创造物苦苦等待；
他的信使纷纷而来，
他却没有来到门外。

我两度造出一个形象，
又三次把我的手展开，
造一个用白昼，另一个用夜晚，
还有一个用那盐渍的海滩。

一个在犹大的马槽，
还有一个在埃文河畔，
一个对着尼罗河口，
还有一个在“学苑”。

我造出国王与救世主，
还有王权莫及的游吟诗仙；——
却未能降下灿如群星的感化，
那杯子从未充满。

再次将那些光辉的轮子旋转，
再度混合起杯中诸物；
沸腾吧，命运！远古的元素，
热，冷，湿，干，还有和平，还有痛苦。

让战争、贸易、教义、歌曲

结合，并日臻成熟，
人要抚育被太阳炙灼的世界
每一寸土地，和不可穷尽的年数。

光线不再黯淡，原子不再衰竭，
我亘古的力量完好如新，
鲜艳的玫瑰在远处的荆丛
用露珠透映弯曲的苍穹。

背景知识

拉尔夫 · 瓦尔多 · 爱默生（Ralph Waldo Emerson），美国散文作家、思想家、诗人。他的诗歌、散文独具特色，注重思想内容而没有过分注重词藻的华丽，行文犹如格言，哲理深入浅出，说服力强，且有典型的“爱默生风格”。有人这样评价他的文字“爱默生似乎只写警句”，他的文字所透出的气质难以形容：既充满专制式的不容置疑，又具有开放式的民主精神；既有贵族式的傲慢，更具有平民式的直接；既清晰易懂，又常常夹杂着某种神秘主义。

单词注解

innumerable [i'nju:mərəbl] 无数的；数不清的
deluge ['delju:dʒ] 涌至；大量泛滥
saurian ['sɔ:riən] 蜥蜴的；蜥蜴状的
cascade [kæs'keid] 小瀑布

名句诵读

Mine are the night and morning, The pits of air, the gulf of space, The sportive sun, the gibbous moon, The innumerable days.

I travail in pain for him, My creatures travail and wait; His couriers come by squadrons, He comes not to the gate.

No ray is dimmed, no atom worn, My oldest force is good as new, And the fresh rose on yonder thorn Gives back the bending heavens in dew.

Night on the Prairies

Walt Whitman

Night on the prairies,
The supper is over, the fire on the ground burns low,
The wearied **emigrants** *sleep, wrapt in their blankets;*
I walk by myself—I stand and look at the stars,
which I think now never realized before.

Now I absorb **immortality** *and peace,*
I admire death and test propositions.

How plenteous! how spiritual! how resume!
The same old man and soul—the same old aspirations,
and the same content.

I was thinking the day most splendid
till I saw what the not—day exhibited,
I was thinking this globe enough
till there sprang out so noiseless around me myriads of other
globes.
Now while the great thoughts of space and **eternity** fill me
I will measure myself by them,

And now touch'd with the lives of other globes arrived as far along as those of the earth,
Or waiting to arrive, or pass'd on farther than those of the earth,
I **henceforth** no more ignore them than I ignore my own life,
Or the lives of the earth arrived as far as mine, or waiting to arrive.

O I see now that life cannot exhibit all to me, as the day cannot,
I see that I am to wait for what will be exhibited by death.

草原之夜

瓦尔特·惠特曼

草原的夜晚，
晚餐过了，火在地上轻轻地燃烧，
疲倦了的牧民裹着他们的毯子睡着了，
我独自散步——我站着观望星星，
那些我以前从没有注意过的星星。
现在我想着永生与和平，
我羡慕死亡，我思考各种问题。
多么丰饶！多么崇高！多么简明哟！
同样的老人和灵魂——同样的旧有的渴望，
同样的满足。

我一直以为白天最为光辉灿烂，
直到我看见黑夜所展示的一切，
我一直以为这个地球已经足够，
直到在我的周围无声地涌现出千万个其他的地球
现在空间和永恒的伟大思想己占据了我，
我要以它们来测量我自己，
现在我接触到其他星球的生命，这生命跟地球上的生命一样来

自遥远的地方，

或是即将来临，或是已经超越了地球上的生命，

此后我将不再漠视它们，正如我不漠视我自己的生命，

或者那些在大地上跟我一样到来的，

或将要来到的生命。

啊，我现在知道生命不能向我展示出所有的一切，

白天也不能

我看出我得等待那由死亡展示出来的东西。

背景知识

瓦尔特 · 惠特曼 (Walt Whitman)，美国历史上最伟大的诗人，他创作的《草叶集》代表着美国浪漫主义文学的高峰，是世界文学宝库中的精品。《草叶集》在风格上，惠特曼彻底摈弃了古板的格律，用自由体的形式抒发自由的思想。在写意上，他受当时刚发明的摄影技术的影响，除了追求写真外，一行诗句捕捉一刹即逝的时刻，静态中表现出动感。

《草叶集》问世，代表着诗人思想的转变。草叶既不开花，也不结果，即使任人践踏，任野火燃烧，仍遍布于大地，表现出无限的生命。该诗就出自著名的《草叶集》。

单词注解

emigrant ['emigrənt] 移居的；移民的

immortality [imɔ:'tæləti] 不死，不朽

eternity [i(:)'tə:niti] 永远，永恒

henceforth [hens'fɔ:θ] 今后，从今以后

名句诵读

Night on the prairies, The supper is over, the fire on the ground burns low, The wearied emigrants sleep, wrapt in their blankets; I walk by myself—I stand and look at the stars, which I think now never realized before.

Now I absorb immortality and peace, I admire death and test propositions.

O I see now that life cannot exhibit all to me, as the day cannot, I see that I am to wait for what will be exhibited by death.

A Lane in the Rain

Dai Wangshu

Alone holding an oil–paper umbrella,
I wander along a long
Solitary lane in the rain,
Hoping to encounter
A girl like a bouquet of lilacs
Gnawed by anxiety and resentment.

A girl
The color of lilacs,
The fragrance of lilacs,
The worries of lilacs,
Feeling melancholy in the rain,
Plaintive and hesitating.

Silently she comes closer,
Closer, giving me
A glance like a sigh,
Then she floats past
Like a dream,
Dreary and blank like a dream.

Like a lilac

Floating past in a dream,

the girl floats past me;

Silently she goes further and further,

To the crumbling wall,

Out of the lane in the rain.

In the mournful melody of the rain,

Her color has faded,

Her **fragrance** has disppeared,

Vanished into the void;

Even her glance like a sigh,

Melancholy like lilacs.

Alone holding an oil-paper umbrella,

I wander along a long

Solitary lane in the rain,

Hoping to pass

A girl like a bouquet of lilacs

Gnawed by anxiety and resentment.

雨　巷

戴望舒

撑着油纸伞，独自
彷徨在悠长，悠长
又寂寥的雨巷，
我希望逢着
一个丁香一样的
结着愁怨的姑娘。

她是有
丁香一样的颜色，
丁香一样的芬芳，
丁香一样的忧愁，
在雨中哀怨，
哀怨又彷徨。

她彷徨在这寂寥的雨巷，
撑着油纸伞
像我一样
像我一样地

默默彳亍着，

冷漠，凄清，又惆怅。

她默默地走近

走近，又投出，

太息一样的眼光，

她飘过

像梦一般地

像梦一般地凄婉迷茫。

像梦中飘过

一支丁香地，

我身旁飘过这女郎；

她静默地远了，远了，

到了颓圮的篱墙，

走尽这雨巷。

在雨的哀曲里，

消了她的颜色，

散了她的芬芳，

消散了，甚至她的

太息般的眼光，

丁香般的惆怅。

撑着油纸伞，独自

彷徨在悠长，悠长

又寂寥的雨巷，

我希望飘过

一个丁香一样的

结着愁怨的姑娘。

背景知识

戴望舒（1905 ~ 1950），现代诗人，又称“雨巷诗人”，中国现代派象征主义诗人。戴望舒为笔名，原名戴朝安。 戴望舒的诗歌主要受中国古典诗歌和法国象征主义诗人影响较大，前者如晚唐温庭筠、李商隐，后者如魏尔伦、果尔蒙、耶麦等，作为现代派新诗的举旗人，无论理论还是创作实践，都对中国新诗的发展产生过相当大的影响。

这首诗写于 1927 年夏天。当时中国处于白色恐怖之中，戴望舒因曾参加进步活动而不得不避居于松江的友人家中，在孤寂中咀嚼着大革命失败后的幻灭与痛苦，心中充满了迷惘的情绪和朦胧的希望。《雨巷》一诗就是他的这种心情的表现，其中交织着失望和希望、幻灭和追求的双重情调。诗中那狭窄阴沉的雨巷，在雨巷中徘徊的独行者，以及那个像丁香一样结着愁怨的姑娘，这些意象又共同构成了一种象征性的意境，含蓄地暗示出作者即迷惘感伤又有期待的情怀，并给人一种朦胧而又幽深的美感。

单词注解

solitary ['sɔlitəri] 单独的，独自的
lilac ['lailək]【植】紫丁香
fragrance ['freigrəns] 芬芳；香味

名句诵读

Alone holding an oil-paper umbrella，I wander along a long Solitary lane in the rain，Hoping to encounter A girl like a bouquet of lilacs Gnawed by anxiety and resentment.

Like a lilac Floating past in a dream，the girl floats past me；Silently she goes further and further，To the crumbling wall，Out of the lane in the rain.

Spring Beauties

Ruth Stone

The abandoned campus,
empty brick buildings and early June
when you came to visit me;
crossing the states **midway**,
the straggled belts of little roads;
hitchhiking with your **portable** *typewriter.*
The campus, an academy of trees,
under which some hand, the wind's I guess,
had **scattered** the pale light
of thousands of spring beauties,
petals stained with pink veins;
secret, blooming for themselves.
We sat among them.
Your long fingers, thin body,
and long bones of improbable genius;
some scattered gene as Kafka must have had.
Your deep voice, this passing dust of **miracles**.
That simple that was myself, half conscious,
as though each moment was a page
where words appeared; the bent hammer of the type

struck against the moving ribbon.
The light air，the restless leaves；
the **ripple** of time warped by our longing.
There，as if we were painted
by some unknown ***impressionist***.

春之美神

露斯 · 斯通

被摈弃的校园，
空空的砖瓦房当六月初
你来看望我；
穿行于州际途中，
束带般的小路伸延，
提着你的便携打字机搭车。
校园，一个树林的学院，
在树下有些，我想是风的手，
已经消散了千百
春之美神的苍白光线，
花瓣染上桃红色的血管；
秘密的，为它们自己开放。
我们坐在它们中间。
你那修长的手指，清瘦的身材，
和未必会是天才的长骨；
一些像卡夫卡肯定有的分散的基因。
你深沉的嗓音，通行奇妙尘间。
单纯如我，神志半醒，

似乎每一瞬间都是词语出现之页；

弯型字锤撞击移动的色带。

清淡的空气，烦躁的树叶；

我们的渴望翘曲起时间的微澜。

在那里，好像我们被

几个无名印象派画家绘入了画面。

背景知识

露斯 · 斯通（Ruth Stone），美国当代著名女诗人。1915 年出生于弗吉尼亚州。2002 年，她的第九卷诗集《邻近的星系》荣获第 53 届被誉为文学奥斯卡奖的美国国家图书奖。后来她又获华莱士 · 史蒂文思奖，获奖金 15 万美元。

单词注解

midway ['mid'wei] 中途的；中间的
portable ['pɔːtəbl] 便于携带的，手提式的；轻便的
scatter ['skætə] 散播；撒播
miracle ['mirəkl] 奇迹；奇迹般的人
ripple ['ripl] 涟漪，细浪
impressionist [im'preʃənist] 印象主义者；印象派作家

名句诵读

The abandoned campus, empty brick buildings and early June when you came to visit me; crossing the states midway, the straggled belts of little roads; hitchhiking with your portable typewriter.

We sat among them. Your long fingers, thin body, and long bones of improbable genius; some scattered gene as Kafka must have had.

There, as if we were painted by some unknown impressionist.

Dream and Poetry

Hu Shi

It's all ordinary experience,
All ordinary images.
By chance they emerge in a dream,
Turning out infinite new ***patterns****.*

It's all ordinary feelings,
All ordinary words.
By chance they ***encounter*** *a poet,*
Turning out infinite new ***verses****.*

Once ***intoxicated****, one learns the strength of wine,*
Once smitten, one learns the power of love:
You cannot write my poems
Just as I cannot dream your dreams.

梦与诗

胡　适

都是平常经验，
都是平常影象，
偶然涌到梦中来，
变幻出多少新奇花样！

都是平常情感，
都是平常言语，
偶然碰着个诗人，
变幻出多少新奇诗句！

醉过才知酒浓，
爱过才知情重；
你不能做我的诗，
正如我不能做你的梦。

背景知识

胡适（1891–1962），安徽绩溪上庄村人。他集现代著名诗人、历史家、文学家和哲学家于一身，且因提倡文学革命而成为新文化运动的领袖之一。

这是一首节奏明快、主题明确的哲理诗。梦和诗是相对独立的概念，也许在一般人看来，找不出任何关联，而在作者眼中，做诗和做梦却是相通的：我做我的诗，你做你梦，只有投身其中，才能体会到乐趣。诗和梦可以相互引用，却不能取而代之。

单词注解

pattern ['pætən] 形态，样式
encounter [in'kauntə] 遭遇（敌人）；遇到
verse [və:s] 诗；韵文
intoxicated [in'tɔksikeitid] 醉了的

名句诵读

It's all ordinary experience，All ordinary images. By chance they emerge in a dream，Turning out infinite new patterns.

It's all ordinary feelings，All ordinary words. By chance they encounter a poet，Turning out infinite new verses.

Once intoxicated，one learns the strength of wine，Once smitten，one learns the power of love：You cannot write my poems Just as I cannot dream your dreams.

Invention

Billy Collins

Tonight the moon is a ***cracker,***
with a bite out of it
floating *in the night.*

and in a week or so
according to the **calendar**
it will probably look

like a silver football,
and nine, maybe ten days ago
it reminded me of a thin bright claw.

But eventually—
by the end of the month,
I reckon—

it will waste away
to nothing,
nothing but stars in the sky,

and I will have a few nights

to myself,

a little time to rest my **jittery** pen.

创　作

比利 · 科林斯

今晚的月亮是块
被咬掉一口的薄脆饼干
飘飘荡荡浮在夜天，

按照日历
约莫一周时间
它看似大概会

像个银色的足球，
而九天，或许十天之前
它使我想起一个薄明的蟹钳。

可渐渐地——
到这个月底
我推断——

它将消瘦至
身影全无

天上只留繁星点点，

而对我自己来说
会有几个夜晚
让我极度紧张的笔得以休闲。

背景知识

比利 · 科林斯（Billy Collins），纽约城市大学莱曼学院英语教授，2001 美国桂冠诗人。在《纽约客》、《巴黎评论》、《美国诗歌评论》、《美国学者》等杂志发表过诗作。主要诗集有《有关天使的问题》、《溺水的艺术》等 15 本。现居纽约萨默斯。约翰 · 厄普代克称他的诗“可爱、清澈、柔和，一贯令人吃惊，比表面上更为严肃。”

单词注解

cracker ['krækə] 薄脆饼干；饼干
float [fləut] 漂浮，浮动
calendar ['kælində] 日历；历书
jittery ['dʒitəri]【口】紧张不安的；神经过敏的

名句诵读

Tonight the moon is a cracker, with a bite out of it floating in the night.

But eventually—by the end of the month, I reckon—

Snow Adopted After the Tune of Chin Yuan Chun

Mao Zedong

North country scene:
A hundred leagues locked in ice,
A thousand leagues of whirling snow.
Both sides of the Great Wall
One single white immensity.
The Yellow River's swift current
Is stilled from end to end.
The mountains dance like silver snakes
And the highlands charge like wax-hued elephants,
Vying with heaven in stature.
On a fine day, the land,
Clad in white, adorned in red,
Grows more enchanting.

This land so rich in beauty
Has made countless heroes bow in homage.
But the monarches, such as
Qinshihuang and HanWudi
Were lacking in literary grace,

The emperors, like Tang Tai-tsung and Sung Tai-tsu

Had little poetry in their souls;

That proud son of Heaven Genghis Khan,

Knew only shooting eagles with bow **outstretched**

All those are past and gone!

For truly great men

Look to this age alone.

沁园春·雪

毛泽东

北国风光，
千里冰封，
万里雪飘。
望长城内外，
惟馀莽莽；
大河上下，
顿失滔滔。
山舞银蛇，
原驰蜡象，
欲与天公试比高。
须晴日，
看红妆素裹，
分外妖娆。

江山如此多娇，
引无数英雄竞折腰。
惜秦皇汉武，
略输文采；

唐宗宋祖，

稍逊风骚。

一代天骄，

成吉思汗，

只识弯弓射大雕。

俱往矣，

数风流人物，

还看今朝。

背景知识

毛泽东（1893–1976），字润之。中国共产党、中国人民解放军和中华人民共和国的主要缔造者和领导人、诗人、书法家。

这首词因雪而得、以雪冠名，却并非为雪所作，而是在借雪言志。它隐藏了太多的秘密，含着无尽的玄机。其中的每一句都意有所指，是诗人所思所想的真实流露，是诗人对许多重大问题给出的回答。其情感之真挚、寓意之深远、哲理之精辟，令人拍案叫绝。

单词注解

immensity [i'mənsiti] 无限；广大；巨大
stature ['stætʃə] 高度
outstretch [aut'stretʃ] 伸出；扩展

名句诵读

North country scene：A hundred leagues locked in ice，A thousand leagues of whirling snow.

This land so rich in beauty Has made countless heroes bow in homage.

For truly great men Look to this age alone.

I Never Saw a Moor

Emily Dickinson

I never saw a ***Moor***—
I never saw the Sea—
Yet know I how the Heather looks
And what a ***Billow*** *be.*

I never spoke with God
Nor visited in Heaven—
Yet certain am I of the ***spot***
As if the Checks were given—

我从未看过荒原

艾米莉·狄金森

我从未看过荒原——
我从未看过海洋——
可我知道石楠的容貌
和狂涛巨浪。

我从未与上帝交谈
也不曾拜访过天堂——
可我好像已通过检查
一定会到那个地方。

背景知识

艾米莉 · 狄金森 (Emily Dickinson)，美国著名女诗人。她年少时热爱大自然，乐于出外游玩，与人交往举止优雅，一度是小城社交界之花。23 岁时，她第一次随父亲远游到华盛顿，在费城邂逅华兹华斯，并深深地爱上了他，但华兹华斯已有妻室，这份感情注定是无望的。归来后，狄金森闭门谢客，终生未嫁。邻居偶尔瞥见她身穿的一袭白袍，称之为“白衣女尼”。

《我从未见过荒原》表现诗人身在贫瘠而风险重重的“人间”，而心在自由美好的“天上”。语言简约；意象实在、清晰，有深度；艺术上涉及宗教，平添魅力，耐人寻味。

单词注解

moor [muə] 荒原；沼泽

billow ['biləu] 巨浪，波涛

spot [spɔt] 斑点，斑块

名句诵读

I never saw a Moor—I never saw the Sea— Yet know I how the Heather looks And what a Billow be.

I never spoke with God Nor visited in Heaven—Yet certain am I of the spot As if the Checks were given—

………… I Love This Land …………

我爱这土地

The Beautiful Lady Yu

Li Yu

Spring flowers and autumn moon—when will they be ended?
How many past events can we tell?
The east wind blew through my small **lodge** *again last night.*
The old country, bathed in a bright moon. Is an overwhelming sight!

Those carved **balustrades**, *those marble terraces—They should still be there.*
Only the rosy cheeks have faded.
How much sorrow and pray, can a person carry?
Like the spring torrent flowing eastward, without **tarry**!

虞美人

李　煜

春花秋月何时了，
往事知多少！
小楼昨夜又东风，
故国不堪回首月明中。

雕栏玉砌应犹在，
只是朱颜改。
问君能有几多愁？
恰似一江春水向东流。

背景知识

李煜 (937 – 978)，五代十国时南唐国君，汉族，在位时间为961—975年，字重光，初名从嘉，号钟隐、莲峰居士。李煜才华横溢，工书善画、能诗擅词、通音晓律，是被后人千古传诵的一代词人。本无心争权夺利，一心向往归隐生活的李煜能登上王位完全是个意外，无奈命运弄人。他也是刻于历史卷宗上的亡国之君。

作为一个“好声色，不恤政事”的国君，李煜是失败的；但正是亡国成就了他千古词坛“南面王”的地位。正所谓“国家不幸诗家幸，话到沧桑语始工”。《虞美人》就是千古传诵不衰的著名诗篇。这首词刻画了强烈的故国之思，取得了惊天地泣鬼神的艺术效果。

单词注解

lodge [lɔdʒ] 旅舍；山林小屋

balustrade [ˌbæləs'treid] 栏杆，扶手

tarry ['tɑːri] 耽搁，迟延

名句诵读

Spring flowers and autumn moon—when will they be ended?How many past events can we tell?The east wind blew through my small lodge again last night.The old country，bathed in a bright moon. Is an overwhelming sight!

Those carved balustrades，those marble terraces—They should still be there.Only the rosy cheeks have faded.How much sorrow and pray，can a person carry?Like the spring torrent flowing eastward，without tarry!

Ulysses

Alfred Tennyson

It little profits that an idle king,
By this still hearth, among these barren crags,
Matched with an aged wife, I mete and dole
Unequal laws unto a **savage** *race,*
That hoard, and sleep, and feed, and know not me.

I cannot rest from travel; I will drink
life to the lees. All times I have enjoyed
Greatly, have suffered greatly, both with those
that loved me, and alone; on shore, and when
Through scudding drifts the rainy Hyades
Vexed the dim sea. I am become a name;
For always roaming with a hungry heart
Much have I seen and known—cities of men
And manners, climates, councils, governments,
Myself not least, but honoured of them all—
And drunk delight of battle with my peers,
Far on the ringing plains of windy Troy.
I am part of all that I have met;
Yet all experience is an arch wherethrough

Gleams that untravelled world whose margin fades
Forever and forever when I move.
How dull it is to pause，to make an end，
To rust unburnished，not to shine in use!
As though to breathe were life! Life piled on life
Were all too little，and of one to me
Little remains；but every hour is saved
From that eternal silence，something more，
A bringer of new things；and vile it were
For some three suns to store and hoard myself，
And this gray spirit yearning in desire
To follow knowledge like a sinking star，
Beyond the utmost bound of human thought.

This is my son，my own Telemachus，
To whom I leave the **scepter** and the isle—
Well-loved of me，discerning to fulfill
This labour，by slow **prudence** to make mild
A rugged people，and through soft degrees
Subdue them to the useful and the good.
Most blameless is he，centered in the sphere
Of common duties，decent not to fail
In offices of tenderness，and pay
Meet adoration to my household gods，
When I am gone. He works his work，I mine.

There lies the port；the vessel puffs her sail；
There gloom the dark，broad seas. My mariners，
Souls that have toiled，and wrought，and thought with me—

That ever with a frolic welcome took
The thunder and the sunshine, and opposed
Free hearts, free foreheads—you and I are old;
Old age hath yet his honour and his toil.
Death closes all; but something ere the end,
Some work of noble note, may yet be done,
Not unbecoming men that strove with Gods.
The lights begin to twinkle from the rocks;
The long day wanes; the slow moon climbs; the deep
Moans round with many voices. Come, my friends.
'Tis not too late to seek a newer world.
Push off, and sitting well in order smite
the sounding furrows; for my purpose holds
To sail beyond the sunset, and the baths
Of all the western stars, until I die.
It may be that the gulfs will wash us down;
It may be that we shall touch the Happy Isles,
And see the great Achilles, whom we knew.
Though much is taken, much abides; and though
We are not now that strength which in old days
Moved earth and heaven, that which we are, we are—
One equal temper of heroic hearts,
Made weak by time and fate, but strong in will
To strive, to seek, to find, and not to yield.

尤利西斯

阿尔弗雷德·丁尼生

一个无所事事的国王没有当头，
安居家中，在这个嶙峋的岛国。
我与年老的妻子相伴，颁布着
各种不同的奖惩法令，治理野蛮的民族，——
他们只知道贮藏食物、吃、睡、收藏，却不知道我是谁。

我不能停歇我的跋涉；我决心
饮尽生命之杯。我曾享受过莫大欢乐，
也尝过不少苦头，
有时与爱我的人在一起，有时却独自一人；不论在岸上还是在海上，
激流滚滚，暴风雨把沉沉大海激得汹涌澎湃，
如今我仅成了一个虚名。
我如饥似渴地漂泊不止，
我已见识了许多民族的城池
各种礼仪、各种气候、各国的议员和政要，
我本人并非举足轻重，而是受到最高礼遇。
在遥远的狂风怒吼的特洛伊战场上，

我曾陶醉于与敌手作战的欢欣。
我本身也是我经历的一部分；
然而，所有的经历都只是一座拱门，
穿过拱门，尚未游历的世界在门外闪光，
而随着我一步一步的前进，
它的边界也不断向后退让。
要是就此停歇，那是何等沉闷无趣，
人如宝刀，不磨砺就要生锈，不使用，就不会发光！
生命岂能等同于呼吸！
几次生命堆起来犹嫌太短，
何况我唯一的生命已余年无多。
唯有从永恒的沉寂之中夺回
每个小时，让每个小时都会曾添更多的收获，
带来新的事物；最可厌的是
把自己长期封存、贮藏起来，
让我灰色的灵魂徒然渴望
在人类思想最远的边界之外
追求知识，就像追求沉没的星星。

这是我的儿子忒勒玛科斯，
我给他留下我的岛国和君权节杖，
我很爱他，他有胆有识，
能胜任这一工作；谨慎耐心地
教化粗野的民族，用温和的步骤
驯化他们，使他们成为有用的良民。
他是无可指责的，他虽年少，

在我离去后他会担起重任，
并对我家的信护神表示崇敬。
他做他的工作，我走我的路。

海港就在那边，海船正扬帆起航，
大海黑暗一片。我的水手们
与我同辛劳、同工作、同思想的人——
对雷电和阳光永远是同等的欢迎。
并用自由的心与头颅来抗争，——
你们和我都已老了，但老年
仍有老年的荣誉、老年的辛劳；
死亡终结一切，但在终点前
我们还能做出一番崇高的事业，
使我们配称为与神斗争的人。
礁石上的灯塔已开始闪烁，
长昼将尽，月亮缓缓爬上天边，
海洋向四周发出各种呻吟。
来吧，朋友们，探寻新的世界
现在为时不晚。开船吧！
坐成排，划破这喧哗的海浪，
我决心驶向太阳沉没的彼方，
超越西方星斗的浴场，至死方止。
也许深渊会把我们吞噬，
也许我们将到达琼岛乐土，
与老朋友阿喀琉斯会晤。
尽管我们被拿走的很多，留下的也不少，

虽然我们的力量已不如当初，

已远非昔日移天动地的雄姿，

但我们还是一如既往，有同样的性情，有同样的雄心

虽被时光和命运摧弱，

但仍有坚强的意志，坚持着

去奋斗、去探索、去寻求，就是不屈服。

背景知识

阿尔弗雷德 · 丁尼生 (Alfred Tennyson)，英国 19 世纪的著名诗人，在世时就获得了极高的声誉。他的诗作题材广泛，想象丰富，形式完美，词藻绮丽，音调铿锵。其 131 首的组诗《悼念》被视为英国文学史上最优秀哀歌之一，因而获桂冠诗人称号。其他重要诗作有《尤利西斯》《伊诺克 · 阿登》和《过沙洲》诗歌《悼念集》等。他深受维多利亚女王的赏识。

这首诗是关于希腊英雄尤利西斯在十年漂泊后回到王位上，但因无所作为而苦闷不已。在强烈的求知欲和冒险精神的驱使下，尤利西斯终于决心召集旧部，抛弃眼前的安宁生活，重新驶向海角天涯，去探索新的世界。在诗中，诗人赞美的实际上不是神话中的英雄，而是当代引起争议的科学精神。丁尼生给传说人物注入了新的生命，使尤利西斯的名字成了境界开阔、探索不止的象征。

单词注解

savage ['sævidʒ] 野性的；凶猛的
scepter ['septə] 权杖，节杖
prudence ['pru:dəns] 精明，深谋远虑
frolic ['frɔlik] 欢乐；嬉戏

名句诵读

It little profits that an idle king, By this still hearth, among these barren crags, Matched with an aged wife, I mete and dole Unequal laws unto a savage race, That hoard, and sleep, and feed, and know not me.

Push off, and sitting well in order smite the sounding furrows; for my purpose holds To sail beyond the sunset, and the baths Of all the western stars, until I die.

Answers

Bei Dao

Cruelty is the ID pass of the cruel,
Honesty the grave stone of the honest.
Look, in the sky plated gold,
crooked reflections of all the dead **float** *around.*

The **glacial** epoch is over,
so why is there ice everywhere?
Good Hope was rounded a long time ago,
so where are these thousands of boats racing on the Dead Sea?

I came into this world
with only blank pages, rope and my fingers;
therefore, before final judgements are given,
I need to speak in all the voices of the **defendants**.

Just let me say, world,
I—don't—believe!
If a thousand challengers are under your feet
count me as challenger one–thousand–and–one.

I don't believe the sky is always blue;
I don't believe it was thunder echoing;
I don't believe all dreaming is false;
I don't believe the dead cannot bring judgement.

If the sea is doomed someday to break its levees
my heart must flood with all the bitter waters.
If the land is destined to form the hills again,
let real human beings learn to choose the higher ground.

The latest, favorable turnings, the twinkling stars
studding the naked sky,
are pictographs five-thousand years old.
They are the eyes of the future staring at us now.

回　答

北　岛

卑鄙是卑鄙者的通行证，
高尚是高尚者的墓志铭，
看吧，在那镀金的天空中，
飘满了死者弯曲的倒影。

冰川纪过去了，
为什么到处都是冰凌？
好望角发现了，
为什么死海里千帆相竞？

我来到这个世界上，
只带着纸、绳索和身影，
为了在审判之前，
宣读那些被判决的声音。

告诉你吧，世界
我—不—相—信！
纵使你脚下有一千名挑战者，

那就把我算作第一千零一名。

我不相信天是蓝的，
我不相信雷的回声，
我不相信梦是假的，
我不相信死无报应。

如果海洋注定要决堤，
就让所有的苦水都注入我心中，
如果陆地注定要上升，
就让人类重新选择生存的峰顶。

新的转机和闪闪星斗，
正在缀满没有遮拦的天空。
那是五千年的象形文字，
那是未来人们凝视的眼睛。

实战提升
Practising & Exercise

背景知识

北岛，原名赵振开，祖籍浙江湖州，生于北京。1969 年当建筑工人，后在某公司工作。80 年代末移居国外。北岛的诗歌创作开始于十年动乱后期，反映了从迷惘到觉醒的一代青年的心声，十年动乱的荒诞现实，造成了诗人独特的冷抒情方式——出奇的冷静和深刻的思辨性。

诗中许多意象具有鲜明的色彩感和强烈的象征性。特别是“死海里千帆相竞”，就是对文革十年群魔乱舞、人妖颠倒、是非不分、白色恐怖、正义不彰的高度概括。诗中最撼人心魄的是诗人对黑暗势力的连珠炮般的轰击，那么激烈而坚定，那一连串“不相信”所代表的正是善良与正义的呼声，也代表了人民的不可欺、历史的大浪淘沙。在诗的最后也表现了诗人对于未来的美好向往，对于人民的坚定信心。

单词注解

float [fləut] 漂浮，浮动
glacial ['gleisjəl] 冰冷的；冷淡的
defendant [di'fendənt]【律】被告
pictograph ['piktəgrɑ:f] 象形文字

名句诵读

Cruelty is the ID pass of the cruel，Honesty the grave stone of the honest. Look，in the sky plated gold，crooked reflections of all the dead float around.

Just let me say，world，I—don't—believe!If a thousand challengers are under your feetcount me as challenger one-thousand-and-one.

I don't believe the sky is always blue；I don't believe it was thunder echoing；I don't believe all dreaming is false；I don't believe the dead cannot bring judgement.

The Second Coming

William Butler Yeats

Turning and turning in the widening ***gyre***
The ***falcon*** *cannot hear the falconer;*
Things fall apart; the centre cannot hold;
Mere ***anarchy*** *is loosed upon the world,*
The blood-dimmed tide is loosed, and everywhere
The ceremony of innocence is drowned;
The best lack all conviction, while the worst
Are full of passionate intensity.

Surely some ***revelation*** *is at hand;*
Surely the Second Coming is at hand.
The Second Coming! Hardly are those words out
When a vast image out of Spritus Mundi
Troubles my sight: somewhere in sands of the desert
A shape with lion body and the head of a man,
A gaze blank and pitiless as the sun,
Is moving its slow thighs, while all about it
Reel shadows of the indignant desert birds.
The darkness drops again; but now I know
That twenty centuries of stony sleep

were **vexed** to nightmare by a rocking cradle,

And what rough beast,

its hour come round at last,

Slouches towards Bethlehem to be born?

基督再临

威廉 · 巴特勒 · 叶芝

猎鹰绕着越来越大的圈子不停地盘旋
再也听不见放鹰人的呼唤;
万物分崩离析;中心难以为系;
世上只落下一盘散沙的无政府主义,
血色迷糊的潮流奔腾汹涌,
天真的仪典,亦已为滔天血浪所湮没;
至善者毫无信心,而至恶者
却躁动不止。

一准是某种启示已近在眼前;
一准是基督再临就在眼前。
基督再临!话未出口,
一个巨大的形象便出现在人们脑际
令我花了眼:在大漠沙海之中,
一个狮身人面的形体,
目光如烈日般茫然而无情。
正缓慢地挪动腿脚,周围环绕着
一群义愤的沙漠鸟的影子。

黑暗再度降临；不过现在我知道
过去两千年岩石般的沉睡
都被摇篮摇成了噩梦般的烦恼，
何等粗野的畜牲，
它的时辰已至，
慵懒地朝伯利恒走去投生。

背景知识

威廉·巴特勒·叶芝(William Butler Yeats)，曾于1923年获得诺贝尔文学奖，获奖的理由是“以其高度艺术化且洋溢着灵感的诗作表达了整个民族的灵魂”。

这首诗作于1921年。根据基督教传说，基督将在世界末日重临人间主持审判。叶芝认为古希腊罗马传下来的西方文明今天已接近毁灭时期，两百年内即将出现一种粗野狂暴的反文明，作为走向另一种贵族文明的过渡。

单词注解

gyre ['dʒaiə] 旋回
falcon ['fælkən] 猎鹰
anarchy ['ænəki] 无秩序；混乱
revelation [ˌrevi'leiʃən] 天启，神示
vexed [vekst] 动荡的

名句诵读

Turning and turning in the widening gyre The falcon cannot hear the falconer; Things fall apart; the centre cannot hold; Mere anarchy is loosed upon the world, The blood-dimmed tide is loosed, and everywhere The ceremony of innocence is drowned; The best lack all conviction, while the worst Are full of passionate intensity.

Surely some revelation is at hand; Surely the Second Coming is at hand.

And what rough beast, its hour come round at last, Slouches towards Bethlehem to be born?

Song of Wisdom

Mu Dan

I have reached illusion's end
In this grove of falling leaves,
Each leaf a signal of past joy,
Drifting sere within my heart.

Some were loves of youthful days?
Blazing meteors in a distant sky,
Extinguished, vanished without trace,
Or dropped before me, stiff and cold as ice.

Some were boisterous friendships,
Fullblown blossoms, innocend of coming fall.
Society dammed the pulsing blood,
Life cast molten passion in reality's shell.

Another joy, the spell of high ideals,
Drew me through many a twisting mile of thorn.
To suffer for ideals is no pain;
But oh, to see them mocked and scorned!

Now nothing remains but **remorse**?
Daily punishment for past pride.
When the glory of the sky stands condemned,
In this wasteland, what colour survive ?

There is one tree that stands alone **intact**,
It thrives, I know, on my suffering's lifeblood.
Its greenshade mocks me ruthlessly !
O wisdom tree ! I curse your every growing bud.

智慧之歌

穆　旦

我已走到了幻想底尽头，
这是一片落叶飘零的树林，
每一片叶子标记着一种欢喜，
现在都枯黄地堆积在内心。

有一种欢喜是青春的爱情，
那是遥远天边的灿烂的流星，
有的不知去向，永远消逝了，
有的落在脚前，冰冷而僵硬。

另一种欢喜是喧腾的友谊，
茂盛的花不知道还有秋季，
社会的格局代替了血的沸腾，
生活的冷风把热情铸为实际。

另一种欢喜是迷人的理想，
他使我在荆棘之途走得够远，
为理想而痛苦并不可怕，

可怕的是看它终于成笑谈。

只有痛苦还在，它是日常生活
每天在惩罚自己过去的傲慢，
那绚烂的天空都受到谴责，
还有什么彩色留在这片荒原？

但唯有一棵智慧之树不凋，
我知道它以我的苦汁为营养，
它的碧绿是对我无情的嘲弄，
我咒诅它每一片叶的滋长。

背景知识

穆旦（1918–1977），原名查良铮，著名诗人、翻译家。他与著名作家金庸（查良镛）为同族的叔伯兄弟，皆属“良”字辈。20 世纪 80 年代之后，许多现代文学专家推其为现代诗歌第一人。穆旦于 20 世纪 40 年代出版了《探险者》、《穆旦诗集》(1939 ~ 1945)、《旗》三部诗集，将西欧现代主义和中国传统诗歌结合起来，诗风富于象征寓意和心灵思辨，是“九叶诗派”的代表诗人。

《智慧之歌》一直被看作是穆旦晚年诗歌中的提纲挈领之作，体现出一种人到暮年的冷静朴素和痛苦，读者可以在诗中体察诗人在洞穿人生所有的复杂因素后，达到明净的智慧，但并没有那种看破俗尘、心如死水的消极之意，而是依然坚守信仰。

单词注解

thorn [θɔːn] 刺，棘

remorse [ri'mɔːs] 痛悔；自责

intact [in'tækt] 完整的，未受损伤的

名句诵读

I have reached illusion's end In this grove of falling leaves，Each leaf a signal of past joy，Drifting sere within my heart.

Some were boisterous friendships，Fullblown blossoms，innocend of coming fall.

Its greenshade mocks me ruthlessly！O wisdom tree！I curse your every growing bud .

Convergence of the Twain

(Lines on the loss of the "Titanic")

Thomas Hardy

I

In a **solitude** *of the sea*
Deep from human vanity,
And the Pride of Life that planned her, stilly couches she.

II

Steel chambers, late the **pyres**
Of her salamandrine fires,
Cold currents thrid, and turn to rhythmic tidal lyres.

III

Over the mirrors meant
To glass the **opulent**
The sea-worm crawls—grotesque, slimed, dumb, indifferent.

IV

Jewels in joy designed
To ravish the sensuous mind

Lie lightless，all their sparkles bleared and black and blind.

V

Dim moon–eyed fishes near
Gaze at the gilded gear
And query："What does this vaingloriousness down here？" ...

VI

Well：while was fashioning
This creature of cleaving wing，
The Immanent Will that stirs and urges everything

VII

Prepared a sinister mate
For her–so **gaily** great—
A Shape of Ice，for the time fat and dissociate.

VIII

And as the smart ship grew
In stature，grace，and hue
In shadowy silent distance grew the Iceberg too.

IX

Alien they seemed to be：
No mortal eye could see
The intimate welding of their later history.

X

Or sign that they were bent

By paths coincident

On being anon twin halves of one August event,

XI

Till the Spinner of the Years

Said "Now！" And each one hears,

And consummation comes，and jars two hemispheres.

合二为一

（“泰坦尼克”号失事所感）

托马斯 · 哈代

一

远离人间的虚荣

抛开生命的全盛，

她静静的躺在大海的孤独之中。

二

钢铁的房屋，新近的火堆，

她的火如同火舌，

穿透股股冷流，变成富有节奏的琴声般的潮水。

三

在镜子上方

（它用来映照辽阔景象），

海虫蠕行——怪诞、粘滑、无言、冷淡。

四

为了陶醉敏感的心灵
而在喜悦中设计的珍品
无光的躺着，迷糊、黑暗、迟钝。

五

眼睛朦胧的鱼停在附近，
凝视涂上金色的齿轮，
发出“这个豪华巨物在干什么？”的询问……

六

好吧：当正在研制
这破浪而行的物体，
激动的、催促万物的上帝意志

七

为她——如此快乐的巨体——
准备了一个阴险的伴侣——
冰的形象，为了遥远的、分离的时期。

八

随着潇洒的船的形象
优雅地茁壮成长，
冰山也成长在幽暗的寂静的远方。

九

他们似乎显得相异:

没有世间的视力

能看见他们后期历史熔成内在的整体,

十

或表示他们被系于

一致的道路,

形成以后的威严事件的两个分部,

十一

直至“岁月编织者”发出命令:

“好了!”,于是人人听清,

于是终结降临,使两个半球震惊。

背景知识

托马斯·哈代（Thomas Hardy），英国诗人、小说家。他是横跨两个世纪的作家，早期和中期的创作以小说为主，继承和发扬了维多利亚时代的文学传统；晚年以其出色的诗歌开拓了英国20世纪的文学。哈代作为诗人，也颇有声誉。哈代的诗冷峻、深刻、细腻、优美，言简意赅，自成一格，较他的小说更具有现代意识。

《合二为一》是诗人哈代为“泰坦尼克”号失事而作，诗歌表现了诗人关注人类命运的一片真诚，十分富有哲理，反映出哈代诗歌的独特魅力。

单词注解

solitude ['sɔlitju:d] 孤独；隐居
pyre ['paiə] 火葬用的柴堆
opulent ['ɔpjulənt] 富裕的；丰裕的
gaily ['geili] 快乐地；兴高采烈地
anon [ə'nɔn] 立刻

名句诵读

In a solitude of the sea Deep from human vanity，And the Pride of Life that planned her，stilly couches she.

And as the smart ship grew In stature，grace，and hue In shadowy silent distance grew the Iceberg too.

Till the Spinner of the Years Said “Now！” And each one hears，And consummation comes，and jars two hemispheres.

If

Rudyard Kipling

If you can keep your head when all about you
Are losing theirs and blaming it on you;
If you can trust yourself when all men doubt you,
But make allowance for their doubting too;
If you can wait and not be tired by waiting,
Or, being lied about, don't deal in lies,
Or being hated don't give way to hating,
And yet don't look too good, nor talk too wise;

If you can dream—and not make dreams your master;
If you can think—and not make thoughts your aim;
If you can meet with Triumph and Disaster
And treat those two *impostors* just the same;
If you can bear to hear the truth you've spoken
Twisted by knaves to make a trap for fools,
Or watch the things you gave your life to, broken,
And stoop and build'em up with worn-out tools;

If you can make one heap of all your winnings
And risk it on one turn of pitch-and-toss,

And lose, and start again at your beginnings,
And never breathe a word about your loss;
If you can force your heart and nerve and **sinew**
To serve your turn long after they are gone,
And so hold on when there is nothing in you
Except the Will which says to them, "Hold on!"

If you can talk with crowds and keep your **virtue**,
Or walk with Kings—nor lose the common touch,
If neither **foes** nor loving friends can hurt you,
If all men count with you, but none too much;
If you can fill the unforgiving minute
With sixty seconds' worth of distance run,
Yours is the Earth and everything that's in it,
And—which is more—you'll be a Man, my son!

假　如

拉迪亚德 · 吉卜林

假如你能保持冷静，即使众人
都失去理智并且归咎于你，
假如你能保持自信，即使众人
都怀疑你，让所有的怀疑动摇；
假如你能等待而不因此厌烦，
别人骗你，不要因此骗人，
别人憎恨你，也不去憎恨别人，
不要太乐观，不要自以为是；

假如你能寻梦——而不为梦想主宰；
假如你能思考——而不以思索为目标；
假如你能面对成败祸福
而同样视之如骗徒；
假如你听到你的老实话被小人歪曲
去蒙骗愚蠢之辈而尚能心平气和，
或者见到你毕生的事业被毁，
而尚能执起破旧的工具去着手重建；

如果你在赢得无数桂冠之后，

然后孤注一掷再搏一次，

失败过后，东山再起，

不要抱怨你的失败；

假如你能驱使你的心力和精神

在别人走后，长久地坚守阵地，

让你抓牢，尽管你里面已掏空了

只有意志告诉它们：“坚持！”

假如你能与市井之徒交谈而不失于礼，

出入于贵胄之家而不忘苍生黎民，

假如你能尊重人人而不膜拜何人，

既不受制于仇敌亦不受制于亲朋；

假如你能以六十秒长跑去填满

那不可饶恕的一分钟

这个世界的一切都是你的，

更重要的是——孩子——你是个顶天立地的人！

背景知识

拉迪亚德 · 吉卜林（Rudyard Kipling），英国小说家、诗人。吉卜林一生共创作了 8 部诗集，4 部长篇小说，21 部短篇小说集和历史故事集，以及大量散文、随笔、游记等。他的作品简洁凝炼，充满异国情调，尤其在短篇小说方面，是无与伦比的。

这是吉卜林写给他 12 岁的儿子的一首诗，是告诫儿子如何才能经受住人生旅途中可能遇到的种种精神上考验的勉励诗，表达了一位父亲对儿子的深爱和期望。这首诗对当今社会的广大青少年也同样具有指导和激励作用，尤其是在受到种种心理压力时，如果能够去细细体会和认真领悟这首诗的深刻内涵，这种激励作用甚至会成为提高广大青少年心理调控能力而始终保持心理健康的巨大动力。

单词注解

impostor [im'pɔstə] 骗子；冒充者
sinew ['sinju:] 体力，活力，精力
virtue ['və:tju:] 美德，德行
foe [fəu] 敌人，仇敌

名句诵读

Are losing theirs and blaming it on you;

If you can dream—and not make dreams your master; If you can think—and not make thoughts your aim;

If you can make one heap of all your winnings And risk it on one turn of pitch-and-toss, And lose, and start again at your beginnings, And never breathe a word about your loss;

I Love This Land

Ai Qing

If I were a bird,
*I would sing with my **hoarse** voice*
Of this land buffeted by storms,
Of this river **turbulent** with our grief,
Of these angry winds **ceaselessly** blowing,
*And of the **dawn**, infinitely gentle over the woods....*
—Then I would die
And even my feathers would rot in the soil.
*Why are my eyes always **brimming** with tears?*
Because I love this land so deeply....

我爱这土地

艾　青

假如我是一只鸟，
我也应该用嘶哑的喉咙歌唱：
这被暴风雨所打击着的土地，
这永远汹涌着我们的悲愤的河流，
这无止息地吹刮着的激怒的风，
和那来自林间的无比温柔的黎明……
——然后我死了，
连羽毛也腐烂在土地里面。

为什么我的眼里常含泪水？
因为我对这土地爱得深沉……

背景知识

艾青（1910 ~ 1996），现代诗人，原名蒋海澄，浙江金华人。自幼由一位贫苦农妇养育到 5 岁回家。1928 年入杭州国立西湖艺术学院绘画系。翌年赴法国勤工俭学。

从诗歌风格上看，解放前，艾青以深沉、激越、奔放的笔触诅咒黑暗，讴歌光明；建国后，又一如既往地歌颂人民，礼赞光明，思考人生。他的“归来”之歌，内容更为广泛、思想更为浑厚、情感更为深沉、手法更为多样、艺术更为圆熟。

抗日战争爆发后，艾青怀着高昂的爱国热情、同仇敌忾的民族义愤，投身于反侵略的斗争中，他拿起诗笔，写下了许多脍炙人口的优美诗篇，《我爱这土地》就是其中的一首，作于抗战初期，是藉土地激发诗人情绪的代表作。

单词注解

hoarse [hɔ:s] 嘶哑的；粗哑的
turbulent ['tə:bjulənt] 骚动的；混乱的
ceaselessly ['si:slisli] 不停地；持续地
dawn [dɔ:n] 黎明，拂晓
brim [brim] 边，缘；注满

名句诵读

If I were a bird，I would sing with my hoarse voice

And of the dawn，infinitely gentle over the woods....
—Then I would die
And even my feathers would rot in the soil.
Why are my eyes always brimming with tears?
Because I love this land so deeply....

Yet Do I Marvel

Countee Cullen

I doubt not God is good, well–meaning, kind,
And did He stoop to **quibble** *could tell why*
The little buried mole continues blind,
Why flesh that mirrors Him must some day die.
Make plain the reason tortured Tantalus
Is bailed by the **fickle** fruit, declare
If merely brute caprice dooms Sisyphus
To struggle up a never–ending stair.
Inscrutable His ways are, and immune
To **catechism** by a mind too strewn
With petty cares to slightly understand
What awful brain compels His awful hand
Yet do I marvel at this curious thing:
To make a poet black, and bid him sing!

但是我感到惊奇

康蒂 · 卡伦

我不怀疑上帝的仁慈、善良和好意，
但若是他使用遁词便能解释，
为何地下的鼹鼠仍然瞎眼，
为何反映他形象的肉体总有一天要死去，
说明坦塔罗斯受折磨的原因，
是他被变化不定的果子吸引，
阐明是否仅仅因蛮横的任性，
西西弗斯就注定得攀登无限高的阶梯。
上帝之道深奥莫测，
对人们的诘问置之不理，
他们的头脑塞满鸡毛蒜皮
无法理解操纵他巨手的智慧的威力。
但我对这件怪事感到惊奇：
造出黑肤色诗人，令他唱吟！

背景知识

康蒂 · 卡伦（Countee Cullen），生于纽约市，并且在那里成为诗人，获得很多荣誉。早在中学时期他便在全市诗歌比赛中获奖；在纽约大学，他获得一项重要的诗歌创作奖，被选入美国大学优秀生全国性荣誉组织 PBK 联谊会。1925 年卡伦出版第一部诗集《肤色》，蜚声美国诗坛，并成为二十年代哈莱姆文艺复兴的风云人物之一。除了几本诗集，他还写了一部题为《通往天堂的一条路》的小说和几本供儿童阅读的书。1934 年以后卡伦在纽约市初级中学任教。

单词注解

quibble ['kwibl] 遁辞；谬论
fickle ['fikl] 易变的，无常的
inscrutable [in'skru:təbl] 不可理解的；不可思议的
catechism ['kætikizəm]（天主教）教义问答

名句诵读

I doubt not God is good, well-meaning, kind, And did He stoop to quibble could tell why The little buried mole continues blind, Why flesh that mirrors Him must some day die.

Yet do I marvel at this curious thing: To make a poet black, and bid him sing!

A Man and a Woman Sit Near Each Other

Robert Bly

A man and a woman sit near each other, and they do not long
at this moment to be older, or younger, nor born
in any other nation, or time, or place.
They are content to be where they are, talking or not-talking.
Their **breaths** together feed someone whom we do not know.
The man sees the way his fingers move;
he sees her hands close around a book she hands to him.
They obey a third body that they share in common.
They have made a **promise** to love the body.
Age may come, parting may come, death will come.
A man and a woman sit near each other;
as they breathe they **feed** *someone we do not know,*
someone we know of, whom we have never seen.

一男一女促膝而坐

罗伯特·勃莱

一男一女促膝而坐，这样的时刻
他们不会渴求更老或更加年轻，抑或
生在另一个国度、另一个时间或地点。
他们心满意足于此情此景，无论交谈还是沉默。
他俩的呼吸共同为某个我们所不识的人提供养分。
那个男人看着他手指动弹的样子；
他看到她的双手围拢着一本递过来的书。
他们服从着他们共享的另一个身体。
他们早就作出承诺：爱这身体。
年龄会变老，分离会到来，死亡终会降临。
一男一女这样促膝而坐：
他们呼吸时，为我们所不识的人提供养分，
某个我们知道却从未见面的人。

实战提升
Practising & Exercise

背景知识

罗伯特·勃莱（Robert Bly），二十世纪美国后现代主义诗歌流派新超现实主义（又称“深度意象”）的领袖人物。勃莱是影响过大批当代中国青年诗人的美国诗人之一。他提倡“自然语言”，力图返璞归真；他强调诗歌的音乐性和“内在力量”，认为听众和读者与诗歌的相遇就是人与世界的相遇，他还认为现代世界夺走了语言的意义和情感，而诗人的职责就是要将其还原。他力图摆脱理性和学院派传统的钳制，通过引进中国古典诗、拉美诗歌和欧洲超现实主义诗歌而给美国诗坛带来新的活力。

单词注解

breath [breθ] 呼吸，气息
promise ['prɔmis] 承诺，诺言
feed [fi:d] 饲料；牧草

名句诵读

A man and a woman sit near each other，and they do not long at this moment to be older，or younger，nor born in any other nation，or time，or place.

They obey a third body that they share in common.

as they breathe they feed someone we do not know，someone we know of，whom we have never seen.

He Knows He Has Wings

Victor Hugo

What matter it though life uncertain be
To all? What though its goal
Be never reached? What though it fall and **flee**—
Have we not each a soul?
Be like the bird that on a **bough** too **frail**
To bear him **gaily** swings;
He carols though the slender branches fail—
He knows he has wings!

他自知有翅膀

维克多·雨果

何必去管它，人生总是无定？
有什么关系壮志难成？
又何必计较你蹉跌并败奔——
我们岂不是各自有灵魂？
要像那鸟儿在柔弱的枝梢，
经不起它欢乐地跳跃；
虽然那细枝折断了它仍歌唱——
因为它知道自己有翅膀！

实战提升
Practising & Exercise

背景知识

维克多 · 雨果 (Victor Hugo)，法国诗人、剧作家及小说家。19 世纪浪漫主义文学运动领袖，人道主义的代表人物，被人们称为“法兰西的莎士比亚”。 雨果一生写过多部诗歌、小说、剧本，各种散文和文艺评论及政论文章。雨果的创作历程超过 60 年，其作品包括 26 卷诗歌、20 卷小说、12 卷剧本、21 卷哲理论著，合计 79 卷之多，给法国文学和人类文化宝库增添了一份十分辉煌的文化遗产。

单词注解

flee [fli:] 逃，逃走
bough [bau] 大树枝
frail [freil] 易损坏的；不坚实的
gaily ['geili] 快乐地；兴高采烈地

名句诵读

What matter it though life uncertain be to all ?

Have we not each a soul?

He carols though the slender branches fail—
He knows he has wings!

A Farewel to Worldly Joyes

Anne Killigrew

Farewel to **Unsubstantial** *Joyes,*
Ye *Gilded Nothings, Gaudy Toyes,*
Too long ye have my Soul misled,
Too long with Aiery Diet fed:
But now my Heart ye shall no more
Deceive, as you have **heretofore**:
for when I hear such Sirens sing,
Like Ithica's fore - warned King,
With **prudent** *Resolution I*
Will so my Will and Fancy tye,
That stronger to the Mast not he,
Than I to Reason bound will be:
And though your Witchcrafts **strike** *my Ear,*
Unhurt, like him, your Charms I'll hear.

永别了，尘世的欢乐

安妮·基丽格鲁

永别了，空洞的欢乐，你是
涂金的虚无，华丽的玩具，
太久，你使我的灵魂迷途，
太久，给它空气般的米黍：
但是我的心不会再被你迷惑，
虽然以前你曾经迷惑过我：
当我听到这样的塞壬歌唱，
像伊斯卡受到警告的国王，
以谨慎克制的决心，我将
坚决缚住我的意志和想象，
比他把自己缚于桅杆还要紧，
我将使自己钳制于理性：
虽然你的巫术撞击我的耳鼓，
无动于衷，像他，我倾听你的法术。

背景知识

安妮 · 基丽格鲁（Anne Killigrew），来自一个戏剧世家，她父亲、两位叔父、两位堂兄都是剧作家。她自己既是诗人又是画家。作为约克公爵夫人的高级侍女，她的诗常写宫廷生活、她所服侍的公爵夫人及诗歌理论，也写她自己的绘画。安妮 25 岁时死于天花，她的诗歌由她父亲于 1868 年编辑出版。

单词注解

unsubstantial [ˈʌnsəbˈstænʃəl] 无实质的；不切实际的
ye [jiː]【古】你们；你
heretofore [ˈhiətuˈfɔː]【书】直到此时，迄今为止
prudent [ˈpruːdənt] 审慎的，小心的
strike [straik] 打，击，攻击

名句诵读

Farewel to Unsubstantial Joyes，Ye Gilded Nothings，Gaudy Toyes，Too long ye have my Soul misled，Too long with Aiery Diet fed：

for when I hear such Sirens sing，Like Ithica's fore - warned King，With prudent Resolution I Will so my Will and Fancy tye，That stronger to the Mast not he，Than I to Reason bound will be：And though your Witchcrafts strike my Ear，Unhurt，like him，your Charms I'll hear.

The Road Not Taken

Robert Frost

Two roads **diverged** *in a yellow wood,*
And sorry I could not travel both
And be one traveler, long I stood
And looked down one as far as I could
To where it bent in the undergrowth;

Then took the other, as just as fair,
And having perhaps the better claim,
Because it was **grassy** and wanted wear;
Though as for that the passing there
Had worn them really about the same.

And both that morning equally lay
In leaves no step had trodden black.
Oh, I kept the first for another day!
Yet knowing how way leads on to way,
I doubted if I should ever come back.

I shall be telling this with a sigh
Somewhere ages and ages **hence***:*

Two roads diverged in a wood, and
I took the one less traveled by,
And that has made all the difference.

未选择的路

罗伯特 · 弗洛斯特

黄色的树林里分出两条路，
可惜我不能同时去涉足，
我在那路口久久伫立，
我向着一条路极目望去，
直到它消失在丛林深处。

但我却选了另外一条路，
它荒草萋萋，十分幽寂，
显得更诱人，更美丽；
虽然在这条小路上，
很少留下旅人的足迹。

那天清晨落叶满地，
两条路都未经脚印污染。
啊，留下一条路等改日再见！
但我知道路径延绵无尽头，
恐怕我难以再回返。

也许多少年后在某个地方，
我将轻声叹息将往事回顾：
一片树林里分出两条路
而我选择了人迹更少的一条，
从此决定了我一生的道路。

实战提升
Practising & Exercise

背景知识

罗伯特 · 弗洛斯特 (Robert Frost)，20 世纪美国最伟大的诗人之一，和艾略特、庞德、威廉斯、史蒂文斯一起被誉为 20 世纪美国诗坛的五巨擘。与他同时代的诗人相比，弗罗斯特并不多产，更没有直接描绘现代美国社会。然而，他赢得的荣誉超过他同时代的任何一位美国作家：先后四次获普利策诗歌奖，爱默生－梭罗金奖，荣获包括牛津、剑桥在内的多所大学和学院授予的 44 个荣誉学衔。在 75 岁生日之际，美国参议院通过决议向他祝寿，尊其为民族诗人。

在这首诗歌中，诗人感叹人生有许多道路可供选择，但一个人往往只能走一条路，而还有其他许多条路，因为人生短暂而只能放弃。人生道路的选择带有偶然性、随意性，诗人不写已选择的道路，而重在对未选择的道路发出感叹，引起深入思考人生的选择问题。

单词注解

diverge [dai'və:dʒ] 分叉；叉开
grassy ['grɑ:si] 盖满草的；长满草的
hence [hens] 因此；由此

名句诵读

Two roads diverged in a yellow wood, And sorry I could not travel both And be one traveler, long I stood And looked down one as far as I could To where it bent in the undergrowth;

And both that morning equally lay In leaves no step had trodden black. Oh, I kept the first for another day! Yet knowing how way leads on to way, I doubted if I should ever come back.

I shall be telling this with a sigh Somewhere ages and ages hence:
Two roads diverged in a wood, and I took the one less traveled by,
And that has made all the difference.

The Gardener 16

Ranbindranath Tagore

Hands cling to hands and eyes **linger** on eyes,
thus begins the record of our hearts.
It is the moonlit night of March,
the sweet smell of henna is in the air,
my flute lies on the earth neglected
and your garland of flowers is unfinished.
This love between you and me is simple as a song.

Your veil of the saffron colour makes my eyes drunk.
The jasmine wreath that you wove me thrills to my heart like praise.
It is a game of giving and withholding，revealing and screening again；some smiles and some little shyness，
and some sweet useless struggles.
This love between you and me is simple as a song.

No mystery beyond the present；
no striving for the impossible；
no shadow behind the charm；
no groping in the depth of the dark.

This love between you and me is simple as a song.

*We do not **stray** out of all words into the ever silent;*
*we do not raise our hands to the **void** for things beyond hope.*
It is enough what we give and we get.
We have not **crushed** the joy to the utmost to wring from it the wine of pain.
This love between you and me is simple as a song.

园丁集 16

罗宾德拉纳特 · 泰戈尔

两手相挽，凝眸相视，

这样开始了我们的心的记录。

这是三月的月明之夜，

空气里是指甲花的甜香，

我的横笛遗忘在地上，

而你的花环也没有编成。

你我之间的爱情像歌曲般单纯。

你的番红花色的面纱，使我醉眼陶然。

你为我编的茉莉花环使我心震颤，像是受了赞扬一般。

这是一种欲予故夺、欲露故藏的游戏；

有些微笑，有些羞怯，

还有一些甜柔的无用的挣扎。

你我之间的爱情像歌曲般单纯。

没有超越现实的神秘；

没有对不可能的事物的强求；

没有藏在魅力背后的阴影；

也没有在黑暗深处的摸索。
你我之间的爱情像歌曲般单纯。

我们并不背离一切言语而走入永远缄默的歧途；
我们并不向空虚伸手要求超乎希望的事物。
我们所给予的和我们所得到的，都已经足够。
我们不曾过度地耽于欢乐而从中榨出痛苦的醇酒。
你我之间的爱情像歌曲般单纯。

背景知识

罗宾德拉纳特 · 泰戈尔 (Ranbindranath Tagore)，印度著名诗人、作家、艺术家和社会活动家。1913 年获诺贝尔文学奖。泰戈尔是具有巨大世界影响的作家。他共写了 50 多部诗集，被称为“诗圣”。

《园丁集》是泰戈尔的一部重要的代表作，是一部“生命之歌”，它更多地融入了诗人青春时代的体验，细腻地描叙了爱情的幸福、烦恼与忧伤，可以视为一部青春恋歌。诗人在回首往事时吟唱出这些恋歌，在回味青春心灵的悸动时，无疑又与自己的青春保有一定距离，并进行理性的审视与思考，使这部恋歌不时地闪烁出哲理的光彩。

单词注解

linger ['liŋgə] 逗留，徘徊
stray [strei] 迷路，走失；走散
void [vɔid] 空闲的，闲散的
crush [krʌʃ] 压碎，压坏

名句诵读

It is the moonlit night of March；the sweet smell of henna is in the air；my flute lies on the earth neglected and your garland of flowers is unfinished.

We do not stray out of all words into the ever silent；we do not raise our hands to the void for things beyond hope.

This love between you and me is simple as a song.